CRICUT PROJECT IDEAS

An Illustrated Guide to Create Unique and Wonderful Projects. Including Amazing Ideas for Cricut Maker, Explore Air 2, Joy and Tips & Tricks for Beginners and Advanced Users.

Sarah Rose

TABLE OF CONTENTS

Introduction

Perhaps you got a Cricut machine for Christmas or a birthday, yet it's still sitting in its case. On the other hand, possibly you're a devoted crafter searching for a basic device to make creating simpler. Or then again perhaps you've seen huge amounts of cool task pictures on Pinterest and pondered "How do they cut those many-sided structures? I want to do that!" Or perhaps you've known about Cricut, however, you're asking "What is a Cricut machine, and what would you be able to do with it?" Well, you're in the ideal spot; today I will acquaint you with the Cricut Explore Air machine and inform you on all the cool things it can do!

I originally used a Cricut route back in school. I was an RA and our occupant staff office had a Cricut machine and a couple of cartridges that we used for removing letters and shapes to make fun signs and gathering designs. I felt that thing was SO COOL. However, Cricut machines have grown a great deal since I've been in school, and they are considerably cooler at this point!

There are no more cartridges; everything is done carefully so you can use any text style or shape that is on your PC. Also, the majority of the Cricut machines work over Wi-Fi or Bluetooth so that you can plan from your iPhone or iPad, just as from your PC! The Cricut machines are anything but difficult to use, absolutely flexible, and just restricted by your very own imagination!

What is a Cricut Machine?

The Cricut Explore Air is a bite the dust cutting machine (otherwise known as art plotter or cutting machine). You can consider it like a printer; you take a picture or plan on your PC and afterward send it to the machine. As opposed to printing your plan, the Cricut machine removes it from whatever material you need! The Cricut Explore Air can cut paper, vinyl, texture, create froth, sticker paper, false calfskin, and that's only the tip of the iceberg!

When you need to use a Cricut like a printer, it can do that as well! There is an adornment space in the machine, and you can stack a marker in there and afterward have the Cricut "draw" your structure for you. It's ideal for getting a flawless written by hand look if your penmanship isn't too extraordinary.

The Explore arrangement of Cricut machines enables you to get to a colossal advanced library of "cartridges" rather than using physical cartridges, as I did in school. This implies you can use Cricut Design Space (their online plan programming) to take any content or shape from the library and send it to your Cricut to be cut. You can even transfer your structures if you need them!

The Cricut Explore Air can slice materials up to 12″ wide and has a little cutting edge mounted inside the machine. At the point when you're prepared to remove something, you load the material onto a clingy tangle and burden the tangle into the machine. The tangle holds the material set up while the Cricut cutting edge disregards the material and cuts it. At the point when it completes, you empty the tangle from the machine, strip your venture off the clingy tangle, and you're all set!

What Can I Do with A Cricut Machine?

- Cut out enjoyment shapes and letters for scrapbooking

- Make custom, handcrafted cards for any extraordinary event

- Structure a onesie or a shirt

- Make a calfskin arm jewelry

- Make buntings and other gathering beautifications

- Make your own stencils for painting

- Make a vinyl sticker for your vehicle window

- Mark stuff in your storeroom or in a den

- Make monogram cushions

- Make your own Christmas adornments

- Address an envelope

- Brighten a mug, cup, or tumbler

- Engraving glass at home

- Make your own divider decals

- Make a painted wooden sign

- Make your own window sticks

- Cut appliqués or blanket squares

- Make decals for a stand blender

CHAPTER 1:

Projects Design

Machine Reset

When some issues arise with your machine, there might be a need to perform a hard reset for such a problem to be resolved. In performing the hard reset, you are required to take the following steps:

- Turn off the Cricut Explore Air 2 machine.

- Simultaneously hold down the Magnifying glass, pause as well as the power buttons.

- Hold the three buttons down simultaneously until the machine displays a rainbow screen, and you can release the buttons afterward.

- Promptly follow the on-screen instructions that follow.

- Get the process repeated one more time.

How to Start Using the Cricut Machine with No Experience

Crafting is one of the very popular hobbies on earth nowadays. You can discover lots of men, women, and even children who enjoy crafting and some who make a professional living out of it. You will find a lot of unique tools, supplies, and software programs accessible to help these crafting lovers to make the most of their crafts.

The Cricut machine is only that. It is an electronic cutter that helps with newspaper crafts. With just a bit of a button, you can produce lovely designs and get help with aircraft such as home decor, art, paper crafting, and far more. This machine is rather straightforward to navigate and use, so the one thing which you indeed must be worried about is being creative and enabling your creativity run rampant.

There is no need for a computer to use the Cricut apparatus. All you'll need is an ordinary electrical outlet to plug it right into, and you are ready to proceed. Before you start, it is useful to bring a tiny bit of time and make it more familiar with this machine. Take a peek at the newspaper feed to understand how everything works.

The on the button, clip button, and stop button is going to be grouped with the right of the apparatus, the paper feed at the back.

To buy began, first ascertain what crafts you would like to work on. Place a Cricut cartridge into the device, and you get to pick from several designs, dimensions and understand each detail in the manner. There are hundreds and hundreds of possibilities, so the models you can produce with your crafting will be infinite.

There is a user guide that comprises the machine as soon as you purchase it provides a browse in the event you're experiencing some difficulties. Even the Cricut method is a valuable investment for any crafter who selects their hobby thoughtfully.

Making Your First Project Ideas

More and more people are choosing to produce their scrapbooking materials, invitations, and cards. These do-it-yourself options allow a good deal more space for customization in contrast to their mass-created choices. Not only are homemade messages a whole lot more customizable, but they also charge considerably less than a store-bought option. Cricut personal cutting machines also make it feasible for people who have minimum time and even less experience to create professional-looking craft projects anytime.

Cricut cutting machines are available everywhere in craft stores, along with department stores that contain artwork and artwork sections. On the flip side, the very best deals are often located online. For the occasional do-it-yourselfer, the entry-level variation, together with readily available sale prices of roughly $100, is more than sufficient. It is more than capable of creating a massive number of different shape combinations and requires hardly any upkeep. More experienced crafters, or individuals who manage home businesses that produce customized paper products, may find that larger models are more compared with their requirements.

All those machines are automatic and a lot simpler to work with than manual paper cutters. Generally, they can cut through quite heavy paper stock, allowing scrap bookers to produce layouts that have several distinct colors and textures. For information on the best way to use a system, there is a selection of sites offering advice from regular amateur clients. They are a significant source of inspiration and data, demonstrating the method in which the machine could be best used. These sites are an excellent destination for those that are only starting. The very best characteristic of a home Cricut machine would be the capability to make one-of-a-kind pages entirely. Experiment with current form and color combinations to earn something memorable and distinctive.

Cricut cutting machines are adaptable for use for virtually any kind of craft occupation.

Make professional hunting scrapbooks with Cricut personal cutting machines

A circuit cutting machine is also a vital need for any scrap booker. These machines also make it possible for customers to trim the paper into some assortment of fascinating shapes, making personalizing each webpage in a scrapbook easy and pleasurable. Made to be little enough to deliver with you when you journey, they will occupy a small space in your home and might be performed with you for just about any scrapbooking parties you could attend. They are the perfect tool for everyone who is looking for a user-friendly means of producing specific bounds, sew, or other page vases.

Cricut machines can create shapes that are anywhere from 1" to more than 5" tall. Straightforward to change metal cutting patterns have been used to create uniform shapes in many sorts of art paper. These forms might be employed to add custom decoration, joyous shapes, or attractive boundaries that could reflect the material of each page. Card stock of various thickness can be used. Scrap bookers have to be aware that newspaper in a milder tier may cause the blades to be dull quicker. This typically means you need to replace them if necessary, to maintain superior results.

A Cricut machine is not a little investment. Prices start at approximately $100 online, which could place this cutting-edge device out of reach for a few. But when taking under the account, the cost of purchasing packs of pre-cut letters and shapes, most committed scrapbook enthusiasts do find the device will eventually pay for itself. It might also be used for other paper-based crafts, such as making custom invitations, gift tags, and cards. The Cricut Company has an exceptional standing at the trading globe, and their products are going to become lasting; hence no replacement should be needed, despite heavy use.

Scrapbooking is becoming more popular than ever, especially with the guidance of all Cricut capsules. Developing a scrapbook may be fun for the entire family. It is an innovative way to maintain family history with photographs, diary entries, as well as memorabilia. Implementing a Cricut expression cutting machine together with its vast library of Cricut capsules makes pictures previously come home to future generations!

Shortly adhering to the production of photographs, people started creating thoughts of the way to maintain the photos for photos. In the 15th century, as cheap paper became available to the average taxpayer in England, scrapbooks called insignificant books were kept to put away quotes, poetry, and correspondence, along with recipes.

Subsequently, as now, every scrapbook was unique to the author's specific theme. In the 16th century, the friendship files were the rage. These documents were similar to modern-day yearbooks, in which friends signal each other's catalog at the finish of the school year.

All those venomous outlets afforded women in subsequent generations with opportunities to develop their literacy skills by documenting their history. It might be hard for people to imagine now. Still, girls living before the 18th and 19th centuries generally could not read and write made readily available because of them.

The producers of Provo craft certainly do not want to come across these days' returns where women were saved in the dark! They churn out creations all year with every passing year to help make our imagination and imagination to light. For instance, the handy Cricut jukebox was made for scrap bookers to preserve the majority of the Cricut capsules effortlessly handily. Implementing the jukeboxes, there is no need to stop your creative flow if you'd love to modify out cartridges.

Apart from the newly published old west and Hannah Montana, you'll discover beautiful classics such as Disney mickey font cartridge along with Christmas solutions cartridge. Two of my favorites, and that I have been amazed at the results of the task are the home accents solutions cartridge and the home decor solutions cartridge. In the event you've ever wondered precisely what Provo craft suggests by infinite chances in their slogan, peek at those impressive capsules!

Use Your Cricut Machine to Make Money by Scrapbooking

If you're into scrapbooking at all, then surely you have heard about Provo craft's Cricut cutting machines. They are amazing machines that take a fantastic deal of work from a lot of tasks, so they don't require a computer to utilize, plus they are so intuitive and straightforward to comprehend much we can know them! In case you've ever used one, you then almost certainly have noticed precisely how much pleasure they are, but have you ever thought about how to make money doing what you love?

Making money from this flame is a dream of most; however, they usually believe that it's too hard and supply up. The simple fact remains that doing this isn't that difficult! The only limit is your imagination and what it's possible to make. Here's a couple of tips to get you started using wondering how the method to make extra cash with your hobby.

Decorate themed parties

Kids love to own themed celebrations. Whether it is a Pokémon party, a Bakugan birthday party, a Disney character costume celebration, kids simply adore them. You can easily earn some money by producing decoration packs for these kinds of occasions. Print and cut out a great deal of different sized decorations and deliver customized name tags that the kids can adhere, create playing cards as well as character cards which the kids can accumulate and exchange together.

Custom cards and invitations

Who doesn't love a personalized thank you card or invitation? It shows a lot of thought, and love has gone into them. If you adore doing this, why not sell any of the creations to make a little money at precisely the specific same instant? It is astonishing how plenty of people want to obtain a custom-designed card or invite made for birthdays, birthdays, get-togethers, and particular events. Fairly frequently, your neighborhood arts and crafts store is even inclined to put your creations on-screen and market them to get their clientele.

Produce a website

You can consistently promote your products on the internet. Nowadays, it is quite simple to create an internet site. Proceed to blogger.com and enroll to find a free website, then with only a little practice, you will have the ability to generate a superb small website featuring each of the terrific products that you provide. Put it on a business card (also liberated using lots of those online offers in the marketplace) and pass it out to anybody that you meet. They can easily see what you sell and place a purchase.

All these are just a couple of ideas in which you start making money with your hobbies. Don't be intimidated and think you are not good enough or it is too challenging. Just start striving, and you could wind up, amazed at just how good your efforts turn out.

The best idea to use your Cricut on is to make something for your little ones!

Kids love to follow all kinds of stories. However, one story they probably would like to hear repeatedly would be that the narrative of the birth. That's why many might prefer producing baby scrapbook to notify more tangibly about how they appear on earth. But it does not indicate that infant scrapbook is limited to "the way" of giving birth. Even the tiny details are crucial to making a much more impressive baby scrapbook your youngster would enjoy and are very proud of as they grow. And since infant scrapbook is a tiny kid's bibliography, your kids will love exactly how much they mean to you personally.

If you plan to use your Cricut device to make a scrapbook for your baby beforehand, then below are a few things which you have to think about so that you won't confine yourself from creating a baby scrapbook (infant scrapbook that only tells the time, dimensions and burden of your baby).

To make a child scrapbook, you have to define your starting point. It might be the baby shower or maybe the day of their birth. Besides, you ought to set when to complete the scrapbook. Usually, the baby scrapbook will assure the child's very first year. Nonetheless, you might always go longer in case you'd love to. In the process, you want to collect things that might be included on the scrapbook-like the gifts you obtain around your baby shower. Some may even comprise the baby's first haircut together with different events that the child has gotten for the very first moment.

Elect to get a color that will define the subject of the scrapbook. The standard color of a child boy's record is powder blue, while the baby girl's paper is pink. You may choose different colors.

Now you request: "imagine should I comprise from the record?"

Most baby scrapbook could incorporate the truth about the baby upon birth. These are the time of delivery, weight, time of birth, the length of the job, the color of the eyes and hair, and the doctor's name and the names of the group who assisted the doctor in supplying birth. And needless to say, the pictures of you and your child in the hospital after you gave birth.

Some would include pictures of you since you are pregnant. Moments such as this will help keep your child reminded how you personally, as a mother cared for them in your body.

Added seconds you want to add are the photos of the baby's growth month by month employing a measurement reference (generally a stuffed toy), pictures of the house you live in and additionally the nursery, photos of the family members like the baby, pictures of the baby sleeping, photos taken while the baby is bathing, photos together with their favorite toys, and additional joyous moments that comprise them.

As was mentioned before, many baby scrapbooks could include the baby's firsts. These are your baby's first smile, original toilet crawl, opening roster over, initial sat up steps, etc. Baby scrapbook might include their favorites like the favorite song, toys, toys, bedtime stories, along with the shrub.

The beautiful thing about this is that you can always add whatever's connected to your kid as he or she is growing up.

For additional vital events that may or may not be captured by memorabilia could be written.

You may write regarding the significance and worth of the name, your duration of stay from the hospital, added women and men that were present at the hospital, their response once you gave birth, their emotions the moment they completed your baby, and how they entertain the baby. You might even write concerning stories that could further exemplify these events that are listed in photos. Stories like the baby's first flashes, babysitting, along with mannerisms (did he or she often suck their thumb... did the sleep in a funny or cute way).

So, you get the photos and think of what you want to write about them and then just assemble it all in the scrapbook. Creating a scrapbook is particular to parents and different children but just make sure the scrapbook shows how your baby was and how they grew up, following along their journey. Choose the things you would like to add to it.

A few of the advantages of owning the Cricut machine is that it was made for home-use. It is somewhat costly, but worth the expense. My spouse was lucky enough to locate it accessible for 179.99. Provo craft offers a storage tote that has wheels so that you might take it into scrapbook cropping classes or scrapbook parties. It is cartridge-based and has a massive range of fashions of letters, shapes, and phrases to select from — the Cricut cartridges market for around 90.00. The capsules incorporate an overlay that is placed on the Cricut device. These overlays give you a variety of 3d effects. A variety of these is evidence, tags, charms, shadowing, negative, and positive imaging. Everything is right in the touch of a button. It's simply restricted to one's imagination.

You can cut the image as few as 1" as large as 5 1/2". It's possible to use a much different depth of paper, but I have got a propensity to use more of a medium card inventory. The cutting blade is more elastic. There is an anxiety setting for thicker papers. Also, a speed setting for how fast you would like it to cutback. It is an expansion port for future upgrades. The replacement parts for your system are relatively pricey. For example, the cutting mats can be bought 2 in a package for 10.00. The cutting-edge machine won't incorporate all you would like to start. I would need to play around a few with it marginally since there's a learning curve.

You are employing an example for the thinner paper that you want to use the lower speed, or it is going to rip the newspaper. Another example for the thicker paper you're likely to need to correct the blade and put the speed button on a cut. Whenever you are accustomed to it, then it has lots of pleasure to use. I especially love the fact that you are all set to assess the die reductions for secure paper piecing methods. The ideas to get for new scrapbook page layouts are infinite.

A couple of those drawbacks are that you cannot customize your die cuts. You might just use what is on the capsules. The mat which communicates the cutting-edge equipment is tacky. I found the sticky wears off quickly. To use the cloth, I use repositionable spray glue. You are limited to using just real card stock paper. Whatever brand you select. The blade cannot cut any other substances. I like to make chipboard monograms and am unable to use this method.

No wonder that they call it Christmas cheer. This capsule has numerous intriguing shapes that only enable you to feel airy and happy. If you are not in the Christmas spirit, nevertheless, this pill undoubtedly provides you with the jump start that you require. From a smiling reindeer to pieces of candy that you'll be able to decorate your scrapbook pages and cannot miss Santa and his sleigh.

All the Cricut cartridges have work keys; however, the one that I like the maximum with this specific cartridge is the position card feature. All the shapes that are around the capsule are readily available to put on a location card, which makes it perfect for an adult dinner celebration to your child's play celebration. Whatever party that you're having making set cards for your guests will guarantee them to feel special.

There is also a label feature. So that you don't have to purchase gift tags this year for your presents. Just take out this capsule and your favorite paper or ribbon, and then create your own. Now that will save some money too. If you're like me, you wouldn't purchase things like that instead just make them yourself and just consider them your "crafting stash of snacks."

I just thought of a charming idea if you are creating a scrapbook and have a boundary of Christmas lights that are combined with lean decoration. (I would have to do this correctly now) It is possible to have a peek at my site to understand how cute it was, and it only took me about 10 minutes from start to finish. Furthermore, I left Santa a place card to go with his cookies on Christmas eve. You can find dozens of items you'll be able to create with this specific Cricut cartridge. You just require some creativity and a little Christmas cheer to shield you currently crafting!

CHAPTER 2:

Materials You Can Use in the Machine

There are many different materials that the machines can use for any project you desire, and we will be breaking down which machine can use what materials. Something that you should know is that there are materials that the Maker can cut, that the other machines cannot as a matter of fact they include over one hundred different types of fabric.

The official website of the Cricut machines periodically upgrades, in what they say the machines can cut, so as a result you will need to check their website often. In doing so, you will realize what you can still cut even if it may have been taken off the list.

In this section, we will go over a variety of them in detail to get a better understanding of how truly remarkable the Cricut machine really is! Get inspired by a collection of diverse, high-quality materials, all designed to cut perfectly with Cricut machines. Material finishes ranging from fun and flashy, to polished and rich. These materials make it easy to achieve the exact look you want.

Once you get more comfortable using the different types of materials, you will easily be able to create projects that have multiple materials in one. Utilize resources such as this book to refer to, when you have questions relating to what type of material to use and when. The more you know, the better your project will be!

Vinyl

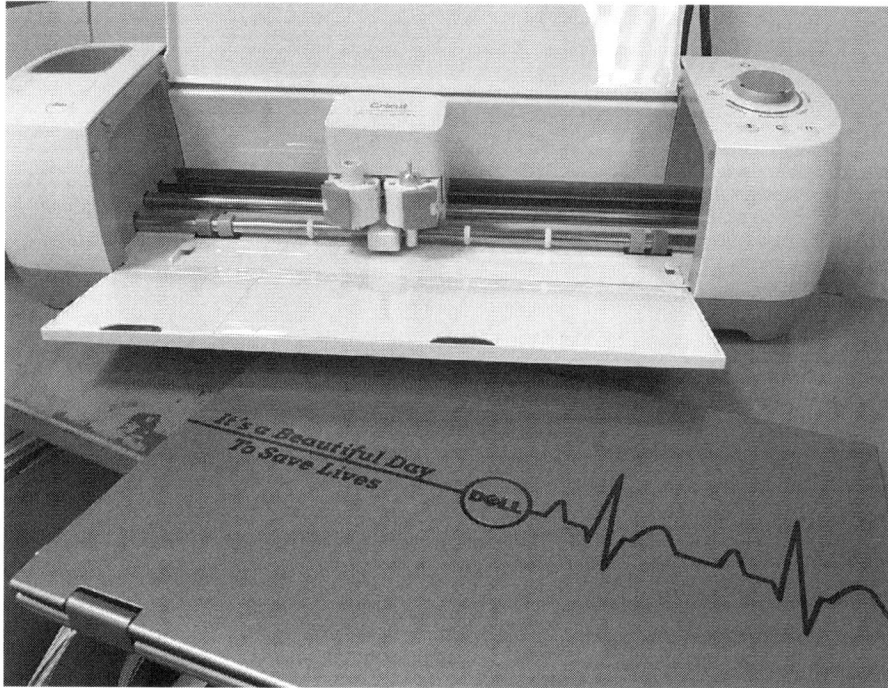

Adhesive vinyl for Cricut cutting machines come in a wide variety of colors, designs, and uses. The adhesive properties can either be semi-permanent (easily removable with adhesive remover), or permanent. Semi-permanent is typically used for indoor projects, such as wall decals or window clings. Permanent vinyl would be used for outdoor use, such as holiday decor and tabletop designs.

Those are perfect for making stickers, indoor and outdoor items, and even 'printing' on mugs and T-shirts. Once you get into it, it is truly addictive to acquire different colors and types. For example, you can get chalkboard vinyl, which is awesome for labeling, or outdoor vinyl, which will look great on your car window. These materials can be purchased at virtually any craft shop, and they are not too expensive if you do a little canvassing. Double check that it is indeed the type of vinyl you are looking for.

Vinyl is the most used material for Cricut projects outside of paper because it is one of the most versatile materials to work with. Adhesive vinyl is a great starting point for creators who are new to Cricut but want to branch outside of paper crafting. Adhesive vinyl is a material that will need to be weeded, as designs are typically cut out of the vinyl and the negative space will need to be removed in order to see the design.

Paper

There is a wide variety of paper products that can be cut using the Cricut machine. Some varieties include cardstock, which is one of the most popular; corrugated cardboard; foil embossed; Kraft board; scrapbooking paper; pearl; sparkle/shimmer; and poster board. Paper products can come in a wide range of sizes, with 12'x12' being the most common and easily applied type as it fits perfectly on a 12'x12' cutting mat.

Paper is most commonly used in card projects, but it can also assist in wall decor, gift boxes, cake toppers and lantern projects. Most crafters familiar with the Cricut recommend starting with the paper project first, to get a handle of the different options Cricut cutters have. Paper allows you to create intricate designs and get familiar with the cutting blade depth at the same time. What you should remember is that you need something to practice on, and a cheap printer paper works wonderfully for that. You will not feel bad for making mistakes because the material does not cost much. If you are feeling more creative than usual, you may get the colored paper too. This way, when you get the hang of cutting, you can create letters for cars or stencils.

The following materials can only be used with the Cricut Maker machine.

Chipboard

The Cricut website sells a variety pack of this type of material, which is great for getting to know the material and what projects to use it for, effectively. It is suggested to be used on projects such as sturdy wall art, school projects, photo frames and more. Since this material has a 1.5mm thickness, it can only be cut using the Cricut Knife blade. Chipboard is great for any type of project that requires dimensions, such as gingerbread, or a haunted house around the holidays!

Fabric

The fabric is great if you have the Cricut Maker. Chances are that you will want to cut some textile with this machine on hand; that is why you should stock up on that and get extra just in case. You can obtain some cheap, scrappy fabrics to practice on before moving on to the proper fabrics for the projects.

This simple, yet classic material, is another favorite among Cricut Maker users. Many use fabrics to create custom clothing, home decor, and wall art. Imagine all the times you went out looking for the perfect top, or skirt only to come back home empty handed after many hours of searching. It would be ideal to find exactly what you want when you want it! Now, without the help of a bulky and outdated sewing machine, you can make simple and affordable clothing exactly the look and feel you want! Fabric is also a great material to make homemade gifts for friends and family. Lots of people enjoy curling up on the couch during the winter months, with a cozy quilt and a favorite movie.

Felt

Blended fibers between natural and synthetic, are also common among craft felts. Felt is commonly used to help young children distinguish among different types of textiles. Felt is also commonly used in craft projects for all ages. The felt is easily cut with your Cricut Machine; no Deep Cut blade required! Felt can be used for: a fun decor, kid's crafts, baby toys, stuffed shapes and more! When starting out on the Cricut Maker, this is one of the best materials to start out with. This material is very forgiving and will allow you to keep the gift-giving spirit going! This material is also great for creating faux flowers. You can bring the outside indoors, without maintenance or worrying about children or pets getting into a mess!

SARAH ROSE

Cardstock

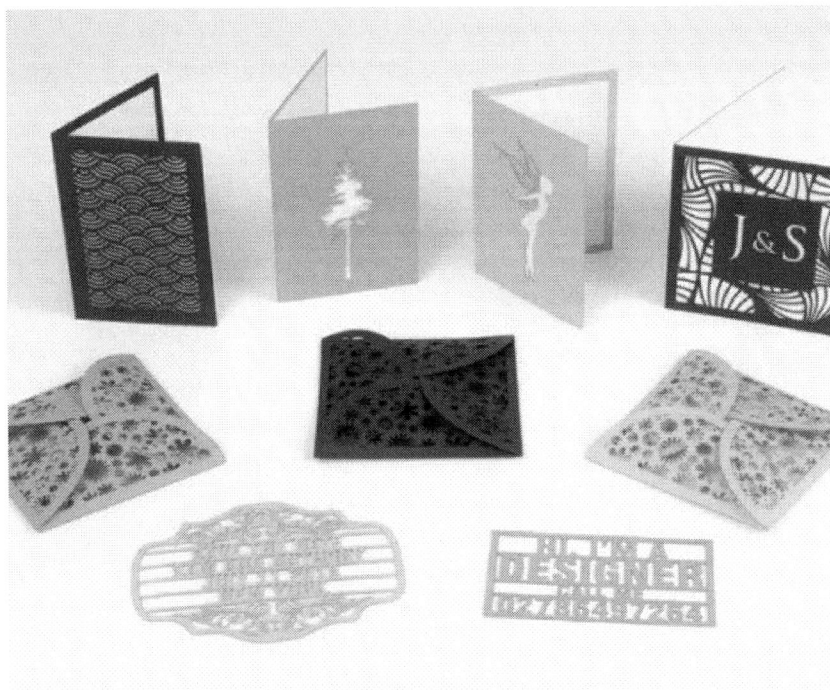

If you plan on making cards or labels, cardstock is a must. The more, the better. It is really awesome to have a large pile of it, and just be able to cut to your heart's content. It will also help practicing, once you have perfected cutting normal printing paper.

Fondant

Fondant is for those bakers out there. There is a possibility that you already have extra fondant lazing about in your home. However, it never hurts to have more. The awesome thing about fondant is that you can reuse it to an extent, depending on how well it freezes or how big the need is to freeze it before cutting. Of course, it is useful to have back up materials for the days that you are in a crafty sort of mood. Most materials are available on the Cricut website, so you can order them along with your Cricut machine. Everything will be delivered at once, and you will not have to buy anything again for a while.

It also depends on what sort of material you will be interested in for creating something awesome. If you are going to cut wood, for instance, you will have to stock up on that as you will be going through it quite fast if you are an enthusiastic and excitable crafter.

The Explore series can only cut certain items and we are going to list them now.

The Explore series can cut these items:

- Tattoo paper
- Washi tape
- Paint chips
- Wax paper
- Faux suede
- Wrapping paper
- Washi paper
- Poster board
- Parchment paper
- Sticker paper
- Construction paper
- Photo paper
- Printable fabric
- Magnetic sheets
- Paper grocery bags
- Craft foam
- Window cling vinyl
- Cardstock
- Flannel
- Vellum
- Duck cloth

- Wool felt

- Cork board

- Tissue paper

- Duct tape

- Matte vinyl

- Iron-on vinyl

- Leather up to 2.0 mm thick

- Sheet duct tape

- Oil cloth

- Soda cans

- Stencil film

- Glitter foam

- Metallic vellum

- Burlap

- Transparency film

- Chipboard that is up to 2.0 mm thick

- Aluminum metal that is up to .14 mm thick

- Stencil vinyl

- Glitter vinyl

- Glossy vinyl

- Faux leather up to 1.0 mm thick

Fabrics, when used with the Explore series, need to be stabilized with *Heat N Bond*. Examples of fabrics are shown on the list below:

- Denim

- Felt

- Silk

- Polyester

Other items that the Explore Series can cut are listed below:

- Chalkboard vinyl

- Adhesive vinyl

- Aluminum foil

- Cardboard

- Stencil film

- Dry erase vinyl

- Printable vinyl

- Outdoor vinyl

- Wood birch up to .5 mm thick

- Cardboard that is corrugated

- Shrink plastic

- Metallic vellum

- White core

- Rice paper

- Photo framing mat

- Pearl cardstock

- Cereal boxes

- Freezer paper

- Iron-on

- Printable iron-on

- Glitter iron-on

- Foil iron-on

- Foil embossed paper

- Neon iron-on

- Matte iron-on

The Maker can cut everything that the Explore series can cut, but it can cut so much more because the Explore series operates with three blades, but the Maker has six. The fact that they have the six blades, enables it to cut more as well as thicker fabric. They also differ from the Explore series in the sense that, the Maker does not have to use *Heat N Bond* to stabilize fabrics. This is a great thing because it means that you can go to a fabric store and choose a fabric, and use it for a project with no preparation, and no additional materials either.

The Maker is also able to utilize the rotary blade as well. This type of blade is new, and it differs from the others that the Explore machines use, because this blade spins, and also twists with a gliding and rolling motion. This rolling action is going to allow the Maker to cut side to side, as well as up and down. Having a blade able to cut any direction is going to help you with the ability to craft great projects. The Maker is even able to cut (up to) three layers of light cotton at the same time. This is great for projects that need uniform cuts.

The Maker is also able to use the knife blade which is a more precise option, and cuts better than the others before it. This blade can cut up to 2.4 mm thick fabric. This machine is also able to use ten times more power to cut, than the others as well.

With that being said, the Maker can cut over a hundred different fabrics that others cannot. We will be listing some of those fabrics below:

- Waffle cloth
- Jacquard
- Gossamer
- Khaki
- Damask
- Faille
- Heather
- Lycra
- Mesh
- Calico
- Crepe paper
- Gauze
- Interlock knit
- Grocery bag
- Acetate
- Chantilly lace
- Boucle
- Corduroy

- EVA foam

- Tweed

- Tulle

- Moleskin

- Fleece

- Jersey

- Muslin

- Jute

- Terry cloth

- Velvet

- Knits

- Muslin

Remember that this is just scratching the surface of what the Maker can cut. There are many other materials as well since the Maker is the ultimate machine and the best out of the four. The Maker is also great for sewing, and there are hundreds of these projects on Design Space. Having a machine that can have access to these projects, and the ability to cut thicker materials means that you have a machine that opens your crafting skills to a whole new level.

CHAPTER 3:

Cricut Projects Ideas to Try

Ideas for "Synthetic Leather Design"

1 Leather Pillow

Leather pillows are great for your holiday décor this year. They will match well with your Christmas tree and other holiday throw pillows. Here's how you can create one by using the Cricut machine.

Here's what you will need: Cricut Explore Air 2, Cricut Design Space, standard cutting mat, ¾ yard of pillow cover in linen-look fabric, white or red, ¼ yard of faux leather, Cricut weeder tool, pillow insert, black heat transfer vinyl, sewing machine with leather sewing needle, thread, iron, fabric shears, heat and bond ultra

1. Open Cricut Design space and create a Christmas tree pattern in the canvas.

You can also upload the Christmas tree and then arrange them in a design on the canvas that would fit your pillow cover.

2. Now it's time for cutting. If your pillow is large, you may have to cut trees in the section, so first decide which of the Christmas trees would be cut from the leather and delete the rest of the trees.

3. Place a heat transfer vinyl onto the cutting mat, then load it into the Cricut machine, set the dial to Faux leather material, and press the cut/go button on the machine to cut trees.

4. When done, cut out the vinyl Christmas trees and then cut a tree from cardstock to use it as a stencil to cut out leather trees by using fabric shears.

5. You can now permanently attach Christmas trees with the help of fabric glue or have them stitch into the pillow cover with matching thread. Make sure your sewing machine is stitching by using a leather sewing needle for this.

6. When done, insert a pillow into the cover and place them as you wanted.

2 <u>Leather Key Ring</u>

Another inexpensive holiday gift is a leather key fob. And the best part, key fobs can be personalized in any way by using Cricut pens. Make a bunch of these rings and give them as gifts and use one for yourself.

Here's what you will need: Cricut Explore Air 2, Cricut Design Space, standard cutting mat, faux leather in brown or blue, Cricut pen in black for personalization, Gorilla glue, keyrings, rivet, paper crafting set, key fob templates

1. Open Cricut Design Space and then open templates for key fobs. You can even use your design and play with them in Design Space.

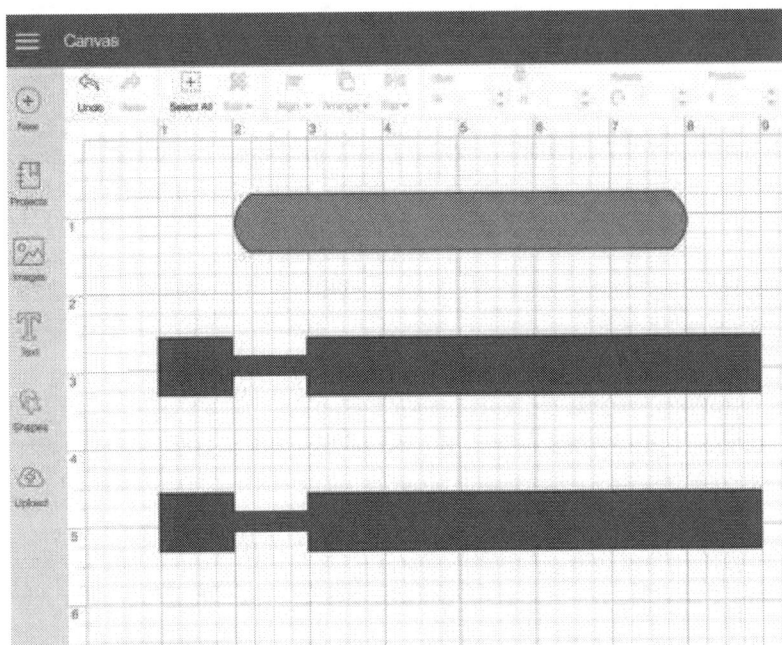

2. Select the designs for key fobs, then load the Cricut machine, set the dial to that Faux leather material, and press the cut/go button on the machine. Insert Cricut pen if you want your designs to be personalized.

3. Use a piercer to poke to fit the rivet, and then slide the keyring onto the key fob. Push the longer end of the rivet through the back of fob, place the rivet mallet on top and then strike it with a handle of a hammer to set it.

And that's it. Here's how your key fob will look.

Here's a challenge for you

Ideas For "Wooden Designs"

3 <u>Wood Christmas Ornaments</u>

Try something new for your Christmas tree or home décor with Cricut Christmas ornaments. There is something special them by making them at home, and they look so pretty and cute, compare to a store-bought set of ornament. Moreover, if you can't find an ornament in the store, you can easily make one.

Here's what you will need: Cricut Explore Air 2, Cricut Design Space, six pieces of a wood slat, acrylic paint, vinyl stencils, foam brush, string, hot glue gun, transfer tape

1. Open Cricut Design Space, begin a new project, and then use Cricut Design Space Image Library to select any image you want to work with. Or you can design the saying in any photo editing program like Adobe Illustrator, and then upload this design into Cricut Design. Make sure to keep the size of the wood slat in mind before designing the sayings.

2. Set the Cricut machine for the "Iron on" setting. You can do this by setting the dial to the "Iron on" position. That's it and leave the rest of the work to the machine.

3. Place a sheet of heat transfer vinyl onto the cutting mat, then load it into the Cricut machine and press the cut button. Make sure the image is in a mirror format as the project deals with heat transfer vinyl.

4. When done, remove the excess vinyl piece from the design by using a Cricut Weeder Tool.

5. You can now apply the vinyl stencil to a raw wood slat, or you can color the slats as well, make sure the slats are dry before using them to create ornaments. You can also cut them into certain shapes to make décor. Apply the created vinyl stencils to the wood slats by using a transfer tape or paper and remove air bubbles by using a smoothing tool.

6. Use a foam brush and acrylic paint to add the first layer of paint, and when it is dried, add the second layer of paint. Before paint gets dry, remove the vinyl stencil.

7. To hang the ornaments, attached a ribbon by using hot glue to wood plaques, and now the ornaments are ready to place.

Ideas For "Etching on Glass and Metal"

Glass application projects are extremely fun and perfect to add some personality to your house and even your car. You will learn to create a variety of projects that you can further customize as you follow the instructions below and have unique designs of your own.

4 Labeling Things in the Pantry

Materials:

- Cricut machine

- Sticker paper

- Inkjet printer

Instructions:

1. Log in to the Cricut design space.

2. Click on the Text icon and input the Jam.

3. Select the font you want to use.

4. Highlight your text and change the color from the ones available on the color tray.

5. Click on the print option and change the file from a cut file to a print file.

6. Highlight the text, ungroup, and adjust the spacing.

7. Highlight the text and group it.

8. Then design the shape of the label.

9. Highlight the text and use the Align drop-down box.

10. Highlight the text and select Move to the Front.

11. Move the text over to the shape.

12. Select both and click on the Group.

13. Highlight the design and click on Attach.

14. Click on the Cricut Go button.

15. Place your sticker paper onto the cutting mat.

16. Load the mat into the machine.

17. Print the design onto the sticker paper.

18. Click the button on the machine to scan the registration and cut.

19. Weed the sticker after cutting.

20. The sticker for labeling jam is ready.

21. Repeat process until all the things in the pantry are labeled.

5 <u>Holiday Mirror Decoration</u>

Materials:

- "Cricut Maker" or "Cricut Explore"

- Cutting mat

- Vinyl

- Transfer tape

- Scrapper

Instructions:

1. Log into the "Design Space" application and click on the "New Project" button on the top right corner of the screen to view a blank canvas.

2. Click on the "Images" icon and type in "reindeer" in the search bar. Select a picture that you like and click on "Insert Image."

3. Now type in "wreath" in the search bar and scroll down to find the image used in this project. Click on it and a small icon will be added to the "Insert Image" bar at the bottom of the screen. Click on "Insert Images" at the bottom of the screen.

4. Edit the design and click on the "Fill" icon from the "Edit Bar" at the top of the screen to select "Print" and then change the color of the deer to red. Click on the lock icon at the bottom left of the deer image to adjust the image inside the wreath.

5. Select the entire design and click on "Group" icon under the "Layers panel." Then click on "Save" to save the project.

6. The design is ready to be cut. Simply click on the "Make It" button and load the vinyl sheet to your "Cricut" machine and follow the instructions on the screen to cut the design.

7. Carefully remove the excess vinyl from the sheet and put the transfer tape on top of the cut design. After you have cleaned the mirror, slowly peel the paper

backing on the vinyl from one end to the other in a rolling motion to ensure even placement. Now, use the scraper tool on top of the transfer tape to remove any bubbles and then just peel off the transfer tape.

6 <u>Wine Glass Decoration</u>

Materials:

1. "Cricut Maker" or "Cricut Explore"

2. Cutting mat

3. Vinyl (gold)

4. Transfer tape

5. Scrapper

6. Wine glasses

Instructions:

1. Log into the "Design Space" application and click on the "New Project" button on the top right corner of the screen to view a blank canvas.

2. Let's use text for this project. Click on "Text" from the "Designs Panel" on the left of the screen and type in "WINE O'clock" or any other phrase you may like.

3. For the image below, the font "Anna's Fancy Lettering–Hannah" in purple, as shown in the picture below, was selected. But you can let your creativity take over this step and choose any color or font that you like. Select and copy-paste your image for the number of times you want to print your design.

4. Click on "Save" to save the project, then click on the "Make It" button and load the vinyl sheet to your "Cricut" machine and follow the instructions on the screen to cut the design.

5. Carefully remove the excess vinyl from the sheet. To easily paste your design on the wine glass without stretching the pieces, put the transfer tape on top of the cut design. After you have cleaned the surface, slowly peel the paper backing on

the vinyl from one end to the other in a rolling motion to ensure even placement. Now, use the scraper tool on top of the transfer tape to remove any bubbles and then just peel off the transfer tape.

7 <u>Window Clings</u>

Materials:

- Window cling
- Cricut machine
- Weeding tool
- Scrapper tool

Instructions:

1. Log in to the Cricut design space.
2. Create a new project.
3. Click on Upload Image.
4. Drag the image to the design space.
5. Highlight the image and "flatten" it.
6. Use the Make It button.
7. Place window a cling to the cutting mat.
8. Custom dial the machine to a window cling.
9. Load the cutting mat into the machine.
10. Push the mat up against the rollers.
11. Cut the design out of the window cling.
12. Weed out the excess window cling.
13. Apply the cut design on the window.
14. Smoothen with a scraper tool to let out all air bubble.

CHAPTER 4:

Step-By-Step Guide on Some Cricut Projects

Easy Project Ideas

8 Mermaid Pillow

Everyone seems really into this kind of design; you can find it everywhere in the store. So, why don't you create it yourself?

Materials:

- Cricut

- Throw Cover Pillow

- Mermaid Set of 2 Blank Pillow Covers

- Iron-On Designs

- Insert 18″ L X 18″ W,

- Household Iron

- Standard / White Cricut Easypress

Instructions:

1. The Cricut Iron-On Designs make it easier to produce lovely t-shirts, pillows, and more. While I love to create using Cricut Design Space, it is a time-saver, and is extremely cost-effective. I discovered this cute Mermaid for just $4.99 in my local craft shop, and they've got so many trendy designs.

2. I followed the Iron-On instructions with my household iron. Just preheat the cotton/linen cover for about 15 seconds. Center the layout and heat each segment for about 50 seconds. Apply medium stress.

3. Let cool for 1-2 minutes, peel the lining back, and be surprised at your lovely picture.

4. Colors are lively. It feels like buying this Mermaid pillow in a fun boutique.

9 Leather Geometric Buffalo Pillo

Simple, easy, but so full of fashion, what else can you ask?

Materials:

- Cricut Maker
- Cricut 12"x 14"
- Cardstock Cricut
- Cutting Mat
- Cricut Fine Point Blade Glue or Tape Runner

Instructions:

1. Resize the flower design to the size you need, and then click "Make It."

2. Once cut, you can collect any parts you want. I hotly attached my toothpicks to the top of my cake. For the term topper, I used bigger wood skewers to stand above the flowers. Instead of flowers, this would be super sweet with mini paper rosettes.

3. Use paper and your Cricut maker to create custom cake decor. With every addition to the tools the maker utilizes, the Cricut Maker has already made it so much easier to create the possibilities.

10   <u>Customized Pillow</u>

A straightforward idea, yet often requested and easy to personalize. Create your ideal pillow!

Materials:

- Protective Sheet Pillow Cover

- Cricut Machine

- Glitter Iron-On Vinyl

- Cricut Easypress Mat

- Insert Cricut Access

- Iron-On

Instructions:

1. Open the Cricut Design Space and click "New Project" from the Home tab.

2. Select the text icon at the lower part of the screen and choose your required font. Type your last name and drag the box corner to make it bigger or lower to suit your pillow

3. Next, pick the Text icon to insert a second line of text for your Est. Year. Drag and center properly under your last name

4. Next, pick both textboxes simultaneously and press the attach button. They appear when you click the Actions button. This will connect the two text boxes for focused cutting.

5. Press the "Make It" button, and the screen appears. You'll want to make sure the Mirror's "on."

6. To switch the mirror environment off and on, press the picture at the top left corner. The screen above appears. Switch the "on".

7. Mirror button: the mat will now display your mirrored picture, and you're prepared to load your Iron-On Vinyl SHINY SIDE DOWN onto your mat. Click and follow the prompts.

8. Once the design is sliced, weed the surplus vinyl and center your pillow cover design.

9. Next, set Easypress timer and temperature for your material. Refer to Easypress Settings Chart.

10. Cover the structure with the Iron-On Protective Sheet and top the protective sheet with the Easypress and click the Cricut button. Remove once it's beeped. Flip through your pillow cover and heat back 10 to 15 seconds.

11. Cool the iron-on and merely remove the sheet.

11 <u>DIY Ice Cream Card</u>

A super-cute project than can highlight every present!

Materials:

- Cardstock in the following colors: Pink, Red, Cream, Tan, and Polka Dot

- Glue Stick Spray

- Scoring Stylus

- Black Cricut Pen

- Adhesive

- Foam Dots

- Double Stick Tape

Instructions:

1. Put the cardstock that controls the cut on the screen on the mat and inserts it into the device. Follow the device prompts and enter the stylus and pen into the adaptive tool system's left side.

2. Now, with all the card elements trimmed, it's time to assemble.

3. Use foam dots or stick tape to connect the ice cream stick inside the cream card.

4. Add spray adhesive or glue stick to the front of the cream card next to the phrases. Attach cherry with a foam dot.

5. Fold the score line card and envelope. Use a stick or double-stick tape to secure the envelope.

6. Now you've produced the first of many Cricut Maker cards to add when you need them.

12 Christmas Tea Towels

Christmas tea towels are a fast and straightforward starting project for the Cricut cutting machine.

Just incorporate heat transfer vinyl, and you can get almost infinite design choices.

Materials:

- A sheet of vinyl heat transfer

- A small towel

- Cricut Explore Air

- Fabric paint

Instructions:

1. Open Cricut Design Space and start a new project.

2. As already mentioned, the Design Space Image Library has over 60,000 pictures, so it's simple to begin designing your project in no time.

3. Select the image you want to work with, and the software will insert it into a new project document. Personally, I some wonderful hand-lettered "Merry and Bright" and "Merry Christmas" designs for my towels and arranged them for vinyl heat transfer sheets.

4. Explore Air's favorite features are dial settings (you don't have to worry about manually changing blade depth or remembering which extent aligns with each material).

5. With Cricut Explore Air, you just turn the knob to grab stuff you're working with, and the machine looks after the straightforward peas.

6. Set "Iron-on" dial, and you're prepared to cut.

7. Place a sheet of vinyl heat transfer, load it into the device, and press the cut button. Use Cricut Weeder to remove the excess vinyl from the design. I put the vinyl on my folded tea towel, covered it with a cloth, and ironed it in the instructions of the package.

8. Once the vinyl heat transfer has been firmly adhered to, you can discard plastic backup. I slipped a piece of cardstock under the towel top and used silver, gold, and champagne-colored fabric paint to add some shiny polka dots. Allow the paint to dry completely before removing the paper layer below.

13 Santa Liners and Envelopes

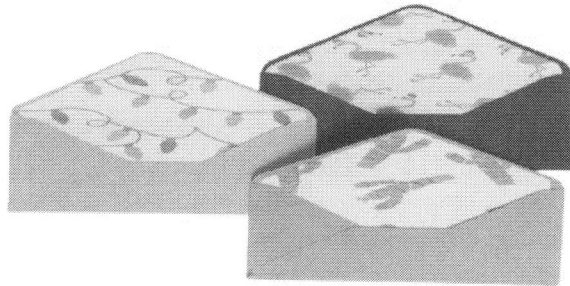

Materials:

- White Card Stock
- Plain White Paper
- Cricut Explore Air
- Light Grip Cutting Mat
- Hot Glue Stick Score Board

Instructions:

1. This Santa Letter Printable Set contains an envelope, a triple letter, and liner cutting file envelope. It's a fun Christmas keepsake.

2. Save Print off the pintable's first page on heavy card stock.

3. Place the page on the light-grip mat. Please make sure you align it as directly as possible, so the graphic appears in the envelope middle.

4. Open the design room and follow THESE directions to upload the SVG envelope file.

5. Cricut Design Space aligns the envelope automatically, so you don't have to. Place it on the page, then press GO.

6. Press the Cricut LOAD button and press that when "C" starts flashing.

7. Once cut, create a score line along with the flaps, and fold in the flaps.

8. Next, print the Liners using THESE directions on plain white paper.

9. Score along the flap, fold inwards.

10. Glue the liner into the envelope using a glue stick

11. Place hot glue in the front and fold the bottom flap inside

12. Print the letter on periodic paper or card stock cut it, and folds along the lines.

13. So, if you generate your printables and want the cut size to be bigger than the permitted quantity, merely align your picture where the file is cut. If you don't cut and print, Cricut will automatically space everything out, starting from top left. You want your picture aligned the same way.

14. Because I had more space for mistakes, I produced this graph very easy. I'm human, so I'm unlikely to align my picture precisely where it is required to be. Since I have no envelope lines, it feels wholly focused.

15. Download Santa Letter Printable: download button make sure you unzip the documents before opening them.

14 Custom Printable Labels

Learn how to create custom printable labels with Cricut machine and then cut the printing function. You can use them to organize supplies of crafts or just anything around your home.

Materials:

- Unfinished wood boxes

- (Natalie Malan Patterned vinyl in Belle Citron

- 4 White chalk paint

- Cricut cut file

- Cricut Printable Vinyl

- (Cricut Explore Air 2 Wild Rose Bundle)

- Paintbrush Cricut Explore Air 2

- Cricut Trimmer

- Supplies required for a wood shelf-organizing craft.

- Painting your shelf and boxes

Instructions:

1. First, painting the shelf and white paint boxes. The boxes come with lids, but I set them aside for another project and used the open-topped boxes as the four fit perfectly on the shelf, adding wood boxes to an organizer's wood shelf.

2. You will then need to offer paint coats to both the shelf and the boxes, painting a white wood shelf for a craft supply organizer.

3. Ensure you paint all surfaces, such as the inside of your boxes and shelf bottom.

4. Paint white wood boxes for craft supplies.

5. Allow drying between coats. I used two surface coats for my project.

6. Add a coat of white chalk to draw boxes.

7. While everything dries, your printable labels can begin. Click here to access the cut file. I already have four labels, but I also have a fifth one that you can use to customize this project. Pick and duplicate all three elements on the fifth label.

8. Then customize print labels in Cricut Design Space.

9. You'll have something to edit then.

10. Customizing printable labels in Cricut Design Space.

11. Pick the text layer and customize it to say whatever you want. You may need to move boxes to make selection simpler. You could alter the font if you wanted to.

12. Then placed all three layers together, choose them all and align them.

13. Using Cricut Design Space align.

14. Click "center" and you'll have another beautiful label, but this time it says whatever you want to say.

15. Click flatten in the bottom right corner to print the label, and it's ready for your device. Be sure to delete any labels before you continue.

16. Now it's time to use print to cut our printable labels. Use Cricut printable vinyl for my labels.

17. Printable vinyl on a Cricut machine.

18. Click "create it" in the design room to print your design once you've printed the picture below. The exterior edge box is for your Cricut machine to find itself. Just place the face on your mat.

19. Use Cricut Explore Air 2 to create printable labels for craft supplies.

20. Customize your dial and select printable vinyl from the custom materials list.

21. Printable label stickers trimmed using the print, and then cut a Cricut machine.

22. PIN The device will first discover the edge, and then cut each label.

23. Printable ornamental labels cut a Cricut using print.

24. You have completely trimmed labels to use on any project.

25. Printable Cricut cutter sticker labels.

26. I was encouraged to add some of the beautiful Natalie Malan florals to my craft space, so I selected my favorite patterned vinyl roll. Hard to choose. You'll also need something to size the vinyl. I'm going to use a trimmer for this, but you could also use a knife and self-healing mat or lay it out in Design Space and use your Cricut device.

27. Supplies required to vinyl wood boxes.

28. Then measure and label length and cut to width.

29. Cutting vinyl with the paper cutter.

30. Peel back and stick straight on your painted wood box.

31. Wrapping boxes in floral vinyl.

32. Use the scraper to smooth the vinyl and remove any bubbles.

33. Smoothing floral vinyl with the scraper.

34. The vinyl won't wrap around these boxes, so I added a second piece to cover them entirely.

35. Adding printed vinyl to box.

36. Then peel off the printable labels and attach it to the front of every boxes to finish your organizer.

37. Adding printable labels to the front of a vinyl-covered box.

38. Your supply organizer will look good with Wild Rose's Cricut Explore Air 2.

39. Cricut Explore Wild Rose Air 2 with a cut craft organizer.

40. You can also decorate your craft space with these custom DIY letter board accessories created from the Natalie Malan materials. I told you I couldn't get enough. You can also watch the video made here.

41. Craft your organizer with printable labels next to a custom accessories letter board.

42. Add whatever craft supplies the organizer wants. Again, you can use this concept to make printable sticker labels for any home space. Make the same kitchen or bathroom organizer.

43. Printable labels for craft supplies including brushes, cutters, washi tape, and pens.

44. The boxes can hold so much, and you can hang on a wall or put it on the counter.

45. Adding craft supplies to a label organizer.

46. With your Cricut machine, printing label stickers are so simple to create and then cut function.

47. DIY shipbuilding with a Cricut Explore Air 2.

48. Use these printable labels to organize your entire home. They're not just for these boxes. On containers, drawers, plastic bins, and so much more.

15 Car Window Decal Sticker

Materials:

- Used Cricut Explore Air

- 2 Premium Outdoor Glossy Vinyl

- Transfer Tape

- Scraper Tool

How to Upload an Image to Cricut Design Space and Create a Cut File:

1. If you don't have a big mouth bass, use Premium Outdoor Glossy Vinyl to transform any cut picture into a window decal. If you want, you can select a photo from Cricut Design Space, but I'll demonstrate how to upload an image and generate your cut file.

2. To discover the ideal picture, simply google search. There are loads of images to choose from, but the simpler the image, the faster it transfers to a cut file. BUT most images will have copyright, and you will be in breach if you use them in any manner for private benefit.

3. When you find your picture, right-click to save it to your laptop. Go to Cricut Design Space, click New Project. Click the Upload button situated at the bottom left.

4. Click Upload Image to drag or drop the picture to the next page.

5. Click the Cricut Design Space Upload button to pick your picture type. For this bass fish, I am keeping it simple, as there aren't various layers of distinct colors.

6. Simply click when selecting the picture type in the Cricut design room now select which picture regions are not part of the final cut. In this situation, I press on white. It transforms into a blue-and-white checkerboard. Click on every white area. Click the fins and tongue in the picture below.

7. Select the picture area to cut the Cricut machine to generate the window decal. Select the picture as a cut picture. This also provides you a preview of how the cut picture looks. There is a back button that you can press to adjust to the image before moving forward.

8. After approving, you are taken back to the initial upload screen, but this time you can see your latest cut file among the pictures.

9. Cut your Cricut Machine Vinyl Decal Click the picture to highlight, and then select Insert Image.

10. To create your vehicle decals, select the picture to put into the canvas. This brings the picture to your design region where you can adjust the image's size or direction. You're prepared to cut.

11. Resize the largemouth bass vehicle window to the size you want it Click on the green button that says "Make It" and obeys the prompts to cut the Cricut Premium Glossy Vinyl picture.

12. After cutting, thoroughly weed or remove the surplus vinyl.

13. Apply a Transfer Tape layer to the cut vinyl. The Transfer Tape will help you position the vinyl without any of the parts stretching or moving out of location.

14. Apply vinyl window transfer paper decal How to Apply a Decal Sticker Clean the window where you want to put the decal well. Then go over again with rubbing alcohol to remove surplus grease or fingerprint smudges.

15. Carefully peel back the vinyl's paperback to allow all elements of the picture release from the sheet.

16. Remove the paper backing from the car window decal to apply the vinyl, begin at one end or corner and roll the vinyl down. This will guarantee even placement.

17. Go over the Scraper Tool Transfer Tape and push any bubbles below the vinyl.

18. Scrape over the vehicle decal when applying the Transfer Tape to a window.

16 Personalized Pillowcase

What would you say to making a personalized pillowcase without actually sewing anything? The best yet is that the Cricut machine will do all the needed cutting. Once again, you are going to be using vinyl to make a lovely personalized item for decorating your home, as a gift for someone you care, or to take a nap! You will find everything you need to start making your personalized pillowcase below.

Materials:

- Iron-on Vinyl

- Pillowcase

- Weeding tool

- Cricut Machine

- Easy Press or iron

Instructions:

1. Upload your preferred design or choose one from the Design Space image library. You can also make your own design. Make sure to adjust the size of the image to the size of the pillow – you don't want the image to be too small, but

you don't also want it to go over the entire surface of the pillow. You can also create a mock-up statement or a witty citation by using a font of your choice. When your design is ready, you can proceed to "Make it" – there you will specify iron-on vinyl as your material of choice. Make sure to use "Mirror" on your design as you will be attaching the image to the pillow. Before you start cutting the image with the machine, set up your cutting mat and arrange the material. Proceed to cut.

2. Your design is cut and now it's the time for weeding. Take your weeding tool and start removing all the excess vinyl from your design until only the image you want on the pillow is left. Remove all vinyl scraps from the working surface and prepare your Easy Press or regular iron. Heat your Easy Press – you can set the timer on. The heating up will take 5 seconds. Afterward, you will heat the pillow surface for 30 seconds before attaching the design to the pillow. Place the vinyl on the pillow where you want the image to be, and then use the Press again. Make sure to apply mild pressure onto the Press and hold for 15 seconds.

3. Let the vinyl piece cool a bit before you remove it from the pillow and reveal your new design. At this moment, the vinyl is too hot and it can burn your fingers. Once the vinyl piece cools down, you can remove it and enjoy your design.

Intermediate Project Ideas

17 Giant Vinyl Stencils

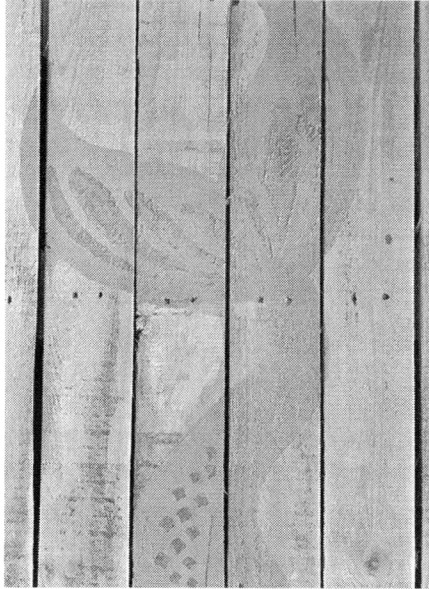

Vinyl stencils are a good thing to create, too, but they can be hard. Big vinyl stencils make for an excellent Cricut project, and you can use them in various places, including bedrooms for kids.

You only need the explore Air 2, the vinyl that works for it, a pallet, sander, and of course, paint and brushes. The first step is preparing the pallet for painting, or whatever surface you plan on using this for.

From here, you create the mermaid tail (or any other large image) in Design Space. Now, you will learn immediately that big pieces are hard to cut and impossible to do all at once in Design Space.

What you do is section of each design accordingly and remove any middle pieces. Next, you can add square shapes to the image, slicing it into pieces so that it can be cut on a cutting mat that fits.

At this point, you cut out the design by pressing *'Make It'*, choosing your material, and working in sections.

From here, you put it on the surface that you are using; piecing this together with each line. You should have one image, after piecing it all together. Then, draw out the line on vinyl, and then paint the initial design. For the second set of stencils, you can simply trace the first one, and then paint the inside of them. At this point, you should have the design finished. When done, remove it very carefully.

And there you have it! Bigger stencils can be a bit of a project, since it involves trying to use multiple designs all at once; but with the right care and the right designs, you will be able to create whatever it is you need to in Design Space, so you can get the results you are looking for.

18 Cricut Quilts

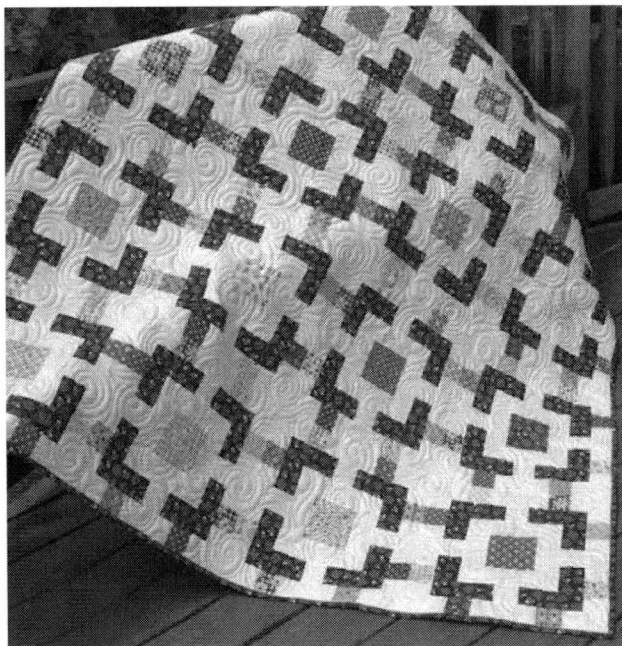

Quilts are a bit hard to do for many people, but did you know that you can use Cricut to make it easier? Here, you will learn an awesome project that will help you do this. To begin, you start with the Cricut Design Space. Here, you can add different designs that work for your project. For example, if you are making a baby blanket, or quilt with animals on it, you can add little fonts with the names of the animals, or different pictures of them too. From here, you want to make sure you choose the option to reverse the design. That way, you will have it printed on correctly. At this point, make your quilt. Do various designs and sew the quilt as you want to.

From here, you should cut it on the iron-on heat transfer vinyl. You can choose that, and then press *'Cut'*. The image will then cut into the piece.

At this point, it will cut itself out, and you can proceed to transfer this with some parchment paper. Use an EasyPress for best results and push it down. There you go, an easy addition that will definitely enhance the way your blankets look.

19 Cricut Unicorn Backpack

If you are making a present for a child, why not give them some cool unicorns? Here is a lovely unicorn backpack you can try to make. To make this, you need ¾ yards of a woven fabric – something that is strong, since it will help with stabilizing the backpack. You will also need half a yard of quilting cotton for the lining. The coordinating fabric should be around about an eighth of a yard. You will need: about a yard of fusible interfacing, some strap adjuster rings, a zipper that is about 14 inches and does not separate, and some stuffing for the horn.

64 | P a g .

To start, you will want to cut the main fabric; you should use straps, the loops, a handle, some gussets for a zipper, and the bottom and side gussets.

The lining should be done too, and you should make sure you have the interfacing. You can use fusible flex foam, to help make it a little bit bulkier.

From here, cut everything and then apply the interfacing to the backside. The flex foam should be adjusted to achieve the bulkiness you are looking for. You can trim this, too. The interfacing should be on the backside; then add the flex foam to the main fabric. The adhesive side of this will be on the right-hand side of the interfacing.

Fold the strap pieces in half and push one down, on each backside. Halve it, and then press it again; stitch these closer to every edge, and also along the short-pressed edge, as well.

From here, do the same thing with the other side, but add the ring for adjustment, and stitch the bottom of these to the main part of the back piece.

Then add them both to the bottom.

At this point, you have the earpieces that should have the backside facing out. Stitch, then flip out, and add the pieces.

Add these inner pieces to the outer ear, and then stitch these together.

At this point, you make the unicorn face in the Design Space. You will notice immediately when you use this program everything will be black, but you can change this by adjusting the desired layers to each color. You can also just use a template that fits, but you should always mirror this before you cut it.

Choose vinyl, and then insert the material onto the cutting mat. From there, cut it and remove the iron-on slowly.

You will need to do this in pieces, which is fine because it allows you to use different colors. Remember to insert the right color for each cut. At this point, add the zipper, and there you go!

20 Custom Back to School Supplies

This tutorial will show you how to use your iPad to create and convert designs for your Cricut machine to cut!

Materials needed:

- Vinyl

- Standard Grip Mat

- White Paper

- Markers (including black)

- Pencil Case

- 3 Ring Binder

- iPad Pro (optional)

- Apple Pencil

- Cricut Design Space App

- Drawing app (e.g. ProCreate)

- ProCreate Brushes

Instructions:

1. The first thing to do is to convert your kid's drawing into an SVG file that the Cricut Design Space recognizes. This will be done by tracing it in the ProCreate app.

2. Get your child's design – it should not be too complex, to minimize weeding.

3. Open the Procreate app on your iPad.

4. Create a new canvas on ProCreate. Click on the 'Wrench' icon and select 'Image'.

5. Next, click 'Take a Photo'. Take a picture of the design. When you are satisfied with the image, click 'Use It'.

6. On the Layer Panel (the two squares icon), add a new layer by clicking the 'plus' sign.

7. In the layers panel, select the layer containing the picture and click the *'N'*. Also, reduce the layer's opacity so that you can easily see your draw lines.

8. From your imported brushes, select the *'Marker'* brush. To avoid the need to import a brush, choose the inking brush. You can resize the brush in the brush settings under the *'General'* option.

9. On the new layer, trace over the drawing.

10. Click on the *'Wrench'* icon, click *'Share'*, then *'PNG'*.

11. Next, *'Save'* the image to your device.

12. Alternately, use your black marker and trace the drawing on a blank piece of paper, then take a picture of it, using your iPad or phone.

13. The next stage is to cut the design out in Cricut Design Space

14. Open the Cricut Design Space app on your iPad.

15. Create a **'New Project'**.

16. Select *'Upload'* (located at the screen's bottom). Select *'Select from Camera Roll'* and select the PNG image you created in ProCreate, or the image you traced out.

17. Follow the next steps.

18. Save the design as a cut file and insert it into the canvas. Here, you can resize the design or add other designs.

19. Next, click *'Make It'* to send it to your Cricut.

20. Choose *'Vinyl'* as the material.

21. Place the vinyl on the mat and use the Cricut to cut it.

Now, you can place the vinyl cutouts on the back, to make your child stand out!

21 Customized Makeup Bag

Materials:

- Pink fabric makeup bag

- Purple heat transfer vinyl

- Cricut EasyPress, or iron

- Cutting mat

- Weeding tool, or pick

- Keychain, or charm of your choice

Instructions:

- Open Cricut Design Space and create a 'New Project'.

- Measure the space on your makeup bag where you want the design and create a box that size.

- Select the 'Image' button in the lower left-hand corner and search *'Monogram'*.

- Choose your favorite monogram and click *'Insert'*.

- Place your vinyl on the cutting mat.

- Send the design to your Cricut.

- Use a weeding tool or pick to remove the excess vinyl from the design.

- Place the design on the bag with the plastic side up.

- Carefully iron on the design.

- After cooling, peel away the plastic by rolling it.

- Hang your charm or keychain off the zipper.

- Stash your makeup in your customized bag!

Advance Project Ideas

22 Felt Roses

Materials:

- SVG files with 3D flower design

- Felt Sheets

- Fabric Grip Mat

- Glue Gun

Instructions:

- First of all, upload your Flower SVG Graphics into the Cricut design space as explained in the "Tips" unit. ("How to import images into Cricut Design Space)

- Having placed the image in the project, select it, right-click and click "Ungroup". This allows you to resize each flower independent of the others. Since you are using felt, it is recommended that each of the flowers are at least 6 inches in size.

- Create several copies of the flowers, as many as you wish, selecting the colors you want in the Color Sync Panel (by dragging and dropping the images on to the color you would want them to be cut on). Immediately you're through with that, click on "Make it" on the Cricut design space.

- Click on "Continue". After your Cricut Maker is connected and registered, under the "materials" options, select "Felt".

- If your rotary blade is not in the machine, insert it on the Fabric Grip Mat, place the first felt sheet (in order of color), then, load them into your Cricut Maker. Press the "cut" button when this is done.

- After they are cut, begin to roll the cut flowers one by one. Do this from the outside in. Make sure that you do not roll them too tight. Use the picture as a guide.

- Apply Hot Glue on the circle right in the middle and press the felt flowers that you rolled up on the glue. Hold this in place and do not let it go until the glue binds it.

- Wait for the glue to dry, and your roses are ready for use.

23 Custom Coasters

Materials:

- Free Pattern Templates

- Monogram Design (in Design Space)

- Cardstock or Printing Paper

- Butcher Paper

- Lint-free towel

- Round Coaster Blanks

- LightGrip Mat

- EasyPress 2 (6″ x 7″ recommended)

- EasyPress Mat

- Infusible Ink Pens

- Heat Resistant Tape

- Cricut BrightPad (optional) for easier tracing

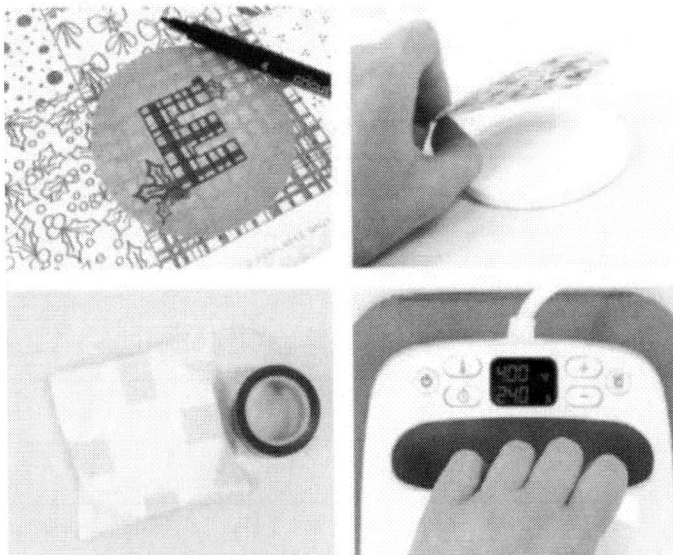

Instructions:

- In Cricut Design Space, open the monogram design. You can click "Customize" and choose the designs that you want to cut out or just go ahead and cut out all the letters.

- Click on "Make It".

- On the page displayed, click on "Mirror Image" to make the image mirrored. This must be done whenever you are using infusible ink. For your material, choose "Cardstock". Then, place your cardstock on the mat and load it into the machine; then press the "Cut" button on the Cricut machine.

- After the Cricut machine is done cutting, unload it and remove the done monograms from the mat.

- Trace the designs onto the cut-out. If you have a Cricut BrightPad, you can use it to carry out this step much more easily, as it will make the trace lines easier to identify. Tracing should be done using Cricut Infusible Ink Pens.

- Use the lint-free towel to wipe the coaster. Ensure that no residue is left behind to prevent any marks being left on the blank.

- Make the design centered on the face down coaster.

- Get a piece of butcher paper which is about an inch larger on each side of the coaster and place on top of the design.

- Tape this butcher paper onto the coaster using heat resistant tape, to hold the design fast.

- Set the temperature of your EasyPress to 400 degrees and set the timer to 240 seconds.

- Place another butcher paper piece on your EasyPress mat, set the coaster on top of it, face up.

- Place another piece of butcher paper on top of these. Place the already preheated EasyPress on top of the coaster and start the timer.

- Lightly hold the EasyPress in place (without moving) or leave it in place right on the coaster – if on a perfectly flat surface – till the timer goes off.

- After this is done, gently remove the EasyPress 2 then turn it off.

- The coaster will be very hot, so you should leave it to cool down before touching. When it is cool, you can peel the design off of it.

24 Customized Doormat

Materials:

- Cricut Machine

- Scrap cardstock (The color does not matter)

- Coir mat (18" x 30")

- Outdoor acrylic paint

- Vinyl stencil

- Transfer tape

- Flat round paintbrush

- Cutting mat (12" x 24")

73 | P a g .

Instructions:

- Create your design in Cricut Design Space. You can also download an SVG design of your choice and import into Cricut Design Space. Make sure that your design is the right size; resize it to ensure.

- Cut the stencil. You do this by clicking "Make it" in Cricut Design Space when you are done with the design. After this, you select "Cardstock" as the material. Then, you press the "Cut" button on the Cricut machine.

- When this is done, remove the stencil from the machine and weed.

- On the reverse side of the stencil, apply spray glue. After this, attach the stencil to the doormat, exactly where you want your design to be; then, pick up the letter bits left on the cutting mat and glue them to their places in the stencil on the doormat.

- The following step is to mask the parts of the doormat which you don't want to paint on. You can do this using painters' plastic.

- Now, it's time to spray-paint your stencil on the doormat. Keeping the paint can about 5 inches away from the doormat, spray up and down, keeping the can pointed straight through the stencil. If it is at an angle, the paint will get under the stencil and ruin your design. Spray the entire stencil 2-3 times to make sure that you do not miss any part and that the paint is even.

- You're just about done! Now, remove the masking plastic and the stencil and leave the doormat for about one hour to get dry.

25 T-Shirts (Vinyl, Iron On)

To make custom t-shirts using your Cricut machine, you will need to use iron-on or heat transfer vinyl. Ensure that you choose a color that contrasts and matches well with your t-shirt.

Materials:

- Cricut Machine

- T-shirt

- Iron on or heat transfer vinyl

- Fine point blade and light grip mat

- Weeding tools

- EasyPress (regular household iron works fine too, with a little extra work)

- Small towel and Parchment paper

Instructions:

- In preparing for this project, Cricut recommends that you prewash the cloth without using any fabric softener before applying the iron-on or heat transfer vinyl on it. Ensure that your T-shirt is dry and ready before you proceed.

- On Cricut Design Space, create your design or import your SVG as described in the unit on importing images.

- If you are using an SVG file, select it and click on "Insert Images". When you do this, the image will appear in the Design Space canvas area.

- Then, you need to resize the image to fit the T-shirt. To do this, select all the elements, then set the height and width in the edit panel area, or simply drag the handle on the lower right corner of the selection.

- After this is done, select all the layers and click "Attach" at the bottom of the "Layers" panel, so that the machine cuts everything just as it is displayed on the canvas area.

- You can preview your design using Design Space's templates. You access this by clicking the icon called "templates" on the left panel of Design Space's canvas. There, you can choose what surface on which to visualize your design. Choose the color of your vinyl and of the T-shirt so you can see how it will look once completed.

- Once you are satisfied with the appearance of your design, click "Make It". If you have not connected your machine, you will be prompted to do so.

- When the "Prepare" page shows, there is a "Mirror" option on the left panel. Ensure that you turn this on. This will make the machine cut it in reverse, as the top is the part that goes on to the T-shirt. Click "Continue".

- Now, select the material. When using the Cricut Maker, you will do this in Cricut Design Space. Choose "Everyday Iron-On". On Cricut Explore Air, you select the material using the smart set dial on the machine. Set this dial to "Iron-On".

- Now, it's time to cut. To cut vinyl (and other such light materials), you should use the light-grip blue mat. Place the iron-on vinyl on the mat with the dull side facing up. Ensure that there are no bubbles on the vinyl; you can do this using the scraper.

- Install the fine point blade in the Cricut machine, then load the mat with the vinyl on it by tapping the small arrow on the machine. Then, press the "make it" button. When the machine is done cutting the vinyl, Cricut Design Space will notify you. When this happens, unload the mat.

- With the cutting done, it is time to weed. This must be done patiently, so that you don't cut out the wrong parts. Therefore, you should have the design open as a guide.

- After weeding, it is finally time to transfer the vinyl to the T-shirt. Before this, ensure that you have prewashed the T-shirt without fabric softener, as mentioned at the beginning of this project.

- To transfer the design, you can use the EasyPress or a regular pressing iron. Using a pressing iron may be a little more difficult, but it is certainly doable. Before you transfer, ensure that you have the EasyPress mat or a towel behind the material on to which you want to transfer the design so as to allow the material to be pressed harder against the heat.

- Set the EasyPress to the temperature recommended on the Cricut heat guide for your chosen heat-transfer material and base material. For a combination of iron-on vinyl and cotton, the temperature should be set to 330ºF. After preheating the EasyPress, get rid of wrinkles on the T-shirt and press the EasyPress on it for about 5 seconds. Then, place the design on the T-shirt and apply pressure for 30 seconds. After this, apply the EasyPress on the back of the T-shirt for about 15 seconds.

- If you're using a pressing iron, the process is similar; only that you need to preheat the iron to max heat and place a thin cloth on the design, such that the iron does not have direct contact with the design or the T-shirt. This will prevent you from burning the T-shirt.

- Wait for the design to cool off a bit, then peel it off while it is still a little warm.

- Ensure that you wait for at least 24 hours after this before washing the T-shirt. When you do wash it, be sure to dry it inside out. Also, do not bleach the T-shirt.

Others Inspirational Project Ideas for the Cricut

26 Coffee Mugs

Arranging gifts for your family, extended family, friends, and relatives can get overwhelming sometimes. But not anymore! Since everyone is a coffee, tea, or hot chocolate lover, so why gift mugs in this holiday season. Read on to know how to make an inexpensive Christmas coffee mugs at home in 10 minutes.

Here's what you will need: Cricut Explore Air 2, Cricut Design Space, black vinyl or silver vinyl, clear transfer tape or paper, coffee mug, "I just want to drink hot cocoa and watch Christmas movies" cut file or "hot chocolate is like a hug from inside" cut file.

1. Open Cricut Design Space. Begin a new project, and then use Cricut Design Space Image Library to select any image you want to work with. Or you can design the saying in any photo editing program like Adobe Illustrator. For example, in this project, I uploaded the design of saying, "I just want to drink hot cocoa and watch Christmas movies." Another example is the saying, "hot chocolate is like a hug."

2. Make sure to adjust the color or material of the design as you like. I use black vinyl for the lettering of "I just want to drink hot cocoa and watch Christmas movies," and silver and silver and red vinyl for the lettering of "I just want to drink hot cocoa and watch Christmas movies." And, then upload I uploaded the design into Cricut Design. Make sure to keep the size of the mug in mind before designing the sayings.

3. Set the Cricut machine for cutting by setting the dial as per the material you are cutting.

4. Place a sheet of heat transfer vinyl onto the cutting mat, then load it into the Cricut machine and press the cut/go button on the machine. Permeant or outdoor vinyl works best for this project as it stays in place after washing.

5. When done, cut the vinyl to remove excess vinyl letting from the design by using a Cricut Weeder Tool.

6. You can now apply the vinyl stencil to a mug of your choice by using transfer tape and remove air bubbles by using a smoothing tool.

27 3D Paper Flowers

Paper flowers are a beautiful way to decorate a gift. Creating paper flowers through the Cricut machine is very easy. Make one flower for a gift or convert it into a bouquet for a larger gift. It's up to you.

The flower for this project is a rolled flower, but you can easily customize the design in Cricut Design Space and mix and match flowers to create flowers of all kinds.

Here's what you will need: Cricut Explore Air 2, Cricut Design Space, Cricut quilling tool, Cardstock, Cricut Standard Grip mat, and glue.

1. Select the image and for this, open Cricut Design space and find the images for flowers in the Flower Shoppe cartridge or simply click on the following link https://design.cricut.com/#/design/new/images/cartridge/288. Scroll the images, select the style of the flower you like, click on insert image, and place it on your canvas. You have ten options for spirals and 40 options for flowers and leaves. Resize the spirals, flowers, and leaves to fit your project.

2. Place cardstock onto the cutting mat, then load it into the Cricut machine, set the dial to that material, and press the cut/go button on the machine to cut spirals.

3. When done, cut out the flower spirals and gently remove them from the mat.

4. Quill the flowers and for this, take the quilling tool, place the end of flower spiral in its slot and then start turning it clockwise to roll spiral. Hold the spiral by placing your index finger under the spiral roll so that the layers aren't disturbed.

5. Place a drop of glue on the circle in the middle of spiral, place the rolled flower on it, let it open slightly, and press flower for a minute or two until the glue holds it.

And now you have your very own paper flower.

Feel free to customize them according to your requirements. The following are great options.

28 Motivational Water Bottle

Everyone needs a motivational boost to keep their workouts going. Turn a boring water bottle into your personal cheerleader! Choose the type of water bottle that you like the best, whether it's a plastic, glass, or metal one. This could also work on a reusable tumbler if you prefer to have a straw. The glitter vinyl will give a fun accent to your necessary hydration, but you can change it to a regular color if you want to be a bit less flashy. Use one of the suggested quotes or one of your own. The important thing is that it motivates you to keep moving! You can use the Cricut Explore One, Cricut Explore Air 2, or Cricut Maker for this project.

- Sturdy water bottle of your choice

- Glitter vinyl

- Transfer tape

- Light grip cutting mat

- Weeding tool / pick

1. Measure the space on your water bottle where you want the text and create a box that size.

2. Select the "Text".

3. Choose your favorite font and type the motivational quote you like best.

    a. I sweat glitter

    b. Sweat is magic

    c. I don't sweat, I sparkle

4. Place vinyl on the cutting mat.

5. Use a weeding tool to remove the excess vinyl from the text.

6. Apply transfer tape to the quote.

7. Remove the paper backing from the tape.

8. Place the quote where you want it on the water bottle.

9. Rub the tape to transfer the vinyl to the bottle, making sure there are no bubbles. Carefully peel the tape away.

10. Bring your new water bottle to the gym for motivation and hydration!

CHAPTER 5:

Other Cricut Project

29 Unicorn Wine Glass

Materials:

- Stemless wine glasses

- Outdoor vinyl in the color of your choice

- Vinyl transfer tape

- Cutting mat

- Weeding tool or pick

- Extra fine glitter in the color of your choice

- Mod Podge

Instructions:

1. Open Cricut Design Space and create a new project.

2. Select the "Text" button in the Design Panel.

3. Type "It's not drinking alone if my unicorn is here."

4. Using the dropdown box, select your favorite font.

5. Adjust the positioning of the letters, rotating some to give a whimsical look.

6. Select the "Image" button on the Design Panel and search for "unicorn."

7. Select your favorite unicorn and click "Insert," then arrange your design how you want it on the glass.

8. Place your vinyl on the cutting mat, making sure it is smooth and making full contact.

9. Send the design to your Cricut.

10. Use a weeding tool or pick to remove the excess vinyl from the design. Use the Cricut BrightPad to help if you have one.

11. Apply transfer tape to the design, pressing firmly and making sure there are no bubbles.

12. Remove the paper backing and apply the words to the glass where you'd like them. Leave at least a couple of inches at the bottom for the glitter.

13. Smooth down the design and carefully remove the transfer tape.

14. Coat the bottom of the glass in Mod Podge, wherever you would like glitter to be. Give the area a wavy edge.

15. Sprinkle glitter over the Mod Podge, working quickly before it dries.

16. Add another layer of Mod Podge and glitter, and set it aside to dry.

17. Cover the glitter in a thick coat of Mod Podge.

18. Allow the glass to cure for at least 48 hours.

19. Enjoy drinking from your unicorn wine glass!

30 Clutch Purse

Materials:

- Two fabrics, one for the exterior and one for the interior
- Fusible fleece
- Fabric cutting mat
- D-ring
- Sew-on snap
- Lace
- Zipper
- Sewing machine
- Fabric scissors
- Keychain or charm of your choice Instructions

Directions:

1. Open Cricut Design Space and create a new project.

2. Select the "Image" button in the lower left-hand corner and search for "essential wallet."

3. Select the essential wallet template and click "Insert."

4. Place the fabric on the mat.

5. Send the design to the Cricut.

6. Remove the fabric from the mat.

7. Attach the fusible fleecing to the wrong side of the exterior fabric.

8. Attach lace to the edges of the exterior fabric.

9. Assemble the D-ring strap.

10. Place the D-ring onto the strap and sew into place.

11. Fold the pocket pieces wrong side out over the top of the zipper, and sew it into place.

12. Fold the pocket's wrong side in and sew the sides.

13. Sew the snap onto the pocket.

14. Lay the pocket on the right side of the main fabric lining so that the corners of the pocket's bottom are behind the curved edges of the lining fabric. Sew the lining piece to the zipper tape.

15. Fold the lining behind the pocket and iron in place.

16. Sew on the other side of the snap.

17. Trim the zipper so that it's not overhanging the edge.

18. Sew the two pocket layers to the exterior fabric across the bottom.

19. Sew around all of the layers.

20. Trim the edges with fabric scissors.

21. Turn the clutch almost completely inside out and sew the opening closed.

22. Turn the clutch all the way inside out and press the corners into place.

23. Attach your charm or keychain to the zipper.

24. Carry your new clutch wherever you need it!

31 Buntings and Other Party Decoration

Materials

- Fabric

- Fabric stabilizer

- Ribbon

- Iron-on glitter vinyl

- Fabric adhesive

- Inkjet printer

- Cricut machine

- Weeding tool

- Transfer Tape

- Needle

- Thread

- Fancy multicolored buttons

- Iron

- Grease-proof paper

Directions:

1. Log in to the Cricut design space.

2. Click on Create a New Project.

3. Use the Insert Shape icon to select the basic shape you want the bunting to be in. (I will explain using the star shape.)

4. Highlight and unlock the Padlock at the lower side of the shape.

5. Edit or resize the shape to your content.

6. Copy and paste the shape as much as required by your text.

7. Click on the Text icon.

8. Type in your text: "Happy Birthday."

9. Choose the font that you want the text cut in.

10. Move to the preview screen.

11. Adjust the shapes to the size of your fabric.

12. Apply the fabric to the cutting mat.

13. Push the cutting mat up against the rollers.

14. Load the mat into the machine.

15. Set the cutting dial to custom.

16. Select the fabric setting.

17. Click Go.

18. Cut out your shapes on the fabric.

19. Cut out the shapes on the fabric stabilizer too.

20. Place the iron-on glitter vinyl shiny side down on the cutting mat.

21. Load the mat into the machine.

22. Push the cutting mat against the rollers.

23. Set the dial to iron-on glitter vinyl setting.

24. Cut out your text with the Cricut machine.

25. Unload the mat.

26. Remove the iron-on vinyl.

27. Use the weeding tool to weed out the waste from the vinyl.

28. Apply transfer tape to your vinyl.

29. Cut each letter of the text separately.

30. Glue the fabric shape together with the fabric stabilizer.

31. Ensure there is no air bubble and that the edges do not overlap.

32. Turn down a point of the buntings to make it "hangable."

33. Sew a button each to the turned-down edge of the buntings.

34. Prepress the bunting shape with a medium-heat iron for some seconds.

35. Apply each vinyl letter on each bunting.

36. Place a grease-proof paper on it.

37. Apply a medium-heat iron on it for thirty seconds.

38. Peel away the transfer tape.

39. Reapply the paper and press again with medium heat iron for few seconds.

40. Tie a bow with the ribbon at one end.

41. Thread the ribbon through the turned-down part of the buntings until all the buntings are linked together by the ribbon.

42. Tie the other end of the ribbon to keep the buntings in place.

43. Your buntings are ready to be hanged.

44. To make any other type of buntings requires this same process; the only difference would be the text and shape.

32 Christmas Ornament

Materials:

- Cricut machine

- Cricut glitter vinyl

- Transfer tape
- Scraper tool
- Weeding tool
- Ribbon

Directions:

1. Log in to the Cricut design space and start a new project.
2. Click on the Input icon.
3. Type in your Christmas greetings.
4. Change the text font.
5. Ungroup and adjust the spacing.
6. Highlight and "weld" to design the overlapping letters.
7. Select the parts of the text you do not want as part of the final cut.
8. Readjust the text size.
9. Select the file as a cut file. You will get to preview the design as a cut file.
10. Approve the cut file.
11. The text is ready to cut.
12. Place the vinyl on the cutting mat shiny side down.
13. Load the mat into the machine.
14. Custom dial to vinyl.
15. Cut the image.
16. Use the weeding tool to remove excess vinyl after the image is cut.
17. Apply a layer of transfer tape to the top of the cut vinyl.

18. Peel back the vinyl paperback.

19. Apply the vinyl onto the glass ornament.

20. Go over the applied vinyl with a scraper tool to remove air bubble underneath the vinyl.

21. Slowly peel away the transfer tape from the glass ornament.

33 Tassels

Materials

- 12" x 18" fabric rectangles

- Fabric mat

- Glue gun

Directions:

1. Open Cricut Design Space and create a new project.

2. Select the "Image" button in the lower left-hand corner and search "tassel."

3. Select the image of a rectangle with lines on each side and click "Insert."

4. Place the fabric on the cutting mat.

5. Send the design to the Cricut.

6. Remove the fabric from the mat, saving the extra square.

7. Place the fabric face down and begin rolling tightly, starting on the uncut side. Untangle the fringe as needed.

8. Use some of the scrap fabric and a hot glue gun to secure the tassel at the top.

9. Decorate whatever you want with your new tassels!

34 Monogrammed Drawstring Bag

Materials:

- Two matching rectangles of fabric

- Needle and thread

- Ribbon

- Heat transfer vinyl

- Cricut EasyPress or iron

- Cutting mat

- Weeding tool or pick

Directions:

1. Open Cricut Design Space and create a new project.

2. Select the "Image" button in the lower left-hand corner and search "monogram."

3. Select the monogram of your choice and click "Insert."

4. Place the iron-on material shiny liner side down on the cutting mat.

5. Send the design to the Cricut.

6. Use the weeding tool or pick to remove excess material.

7. Remove the monogram from the mat.

8. Center the monogram on your fabric, then move it a couple of inches down so that it won't be folded up when the ribbon is drawn.

9. Iron the design onto the fabric.

10. Place the two rectangles together, with the outer side of the fabric facing inward.

11. Sew around the edges, leaving a seam allowance. Leave the top open and stop a couple of inches down from the top.

12. Fold the top of the bag down until you reach your stitches.

13. Sew along the bottom of the folded edge, leaving the sides open.

14. Turn the bag right side out.

15. Thread the ribbon through the loop around the top of the bag.

16. Use your new drawstring bag to carry what you need!

35 Paw Print Socks

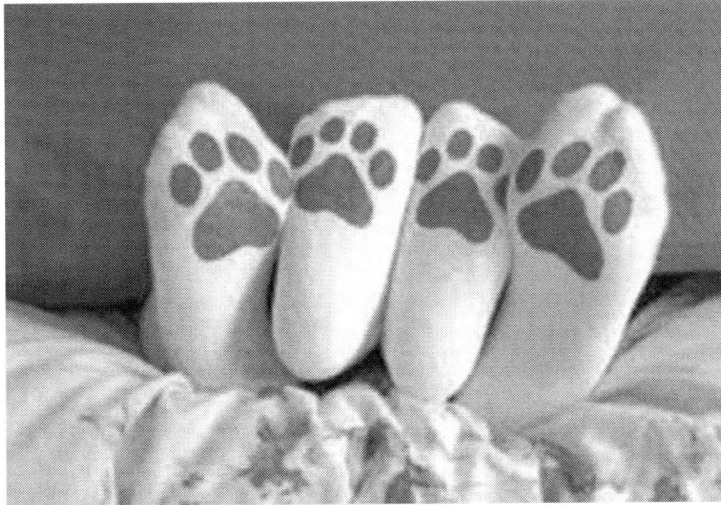

Materials:

- Socks

- Heat transfer vinyl

- Cutting mat

- Scrap cardboard

- Weeding tool or pick

- Cricut EasyPress or iron

Directions:

1. Open Cricut Design Space and create a new project.

2. Select the "Image" button in the lower left-hand corner and search "paw prints."

3. Select the paw prints of your choice and click "Insert."

4. Place the iron-on material on the mat.

5. Send the design to the Cricut.

6. Use the weeding tool or pick to remove excess material.

7. Remove the material from the mat.

8. Fit the scrap cardboard inside of the socks.

9. Place the iron-on material on the bottom of the socks.

10. Use the EasyPress to adhere it to the iron-on material.

11. After cooling, remove the cardboard from the socks.

12. Wear your cute paw print socks!

35 DIY Leather Bow

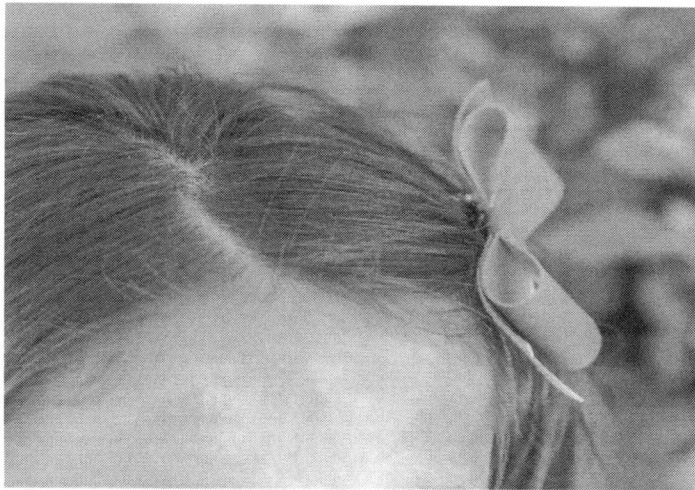

I feel we should really talk some more about children project especially with the use of leather. So, the next project is DIY with Cricut explore leather bows. This is as simple as the key fob.

Materials:

- Leather or Faux Suede. I used the Faux for this project.

- Cricut Explore

- Strong Grip Cricut Mat

- Some Binding Clips

- French Barrette clips

- The Bow Cricut Design space file (not necessary because you can always design yours)

- Transfer Tape

- E6000 Glue

Instructions:

- To the Design space! It is a bow. You should know the shape. Design and measure also.

- Make sure you line your faux suede with the transfer tape. If you're using leather, it is the same process. This process would make the grip of the fabric firm, and it shouldn't leave fuzz all over your mat. You should never stick the fabric on the strong grip mat just like that, you should have something underneath, and that is the transfer tape.

- Pick the faux leather option on your smart dial. This means that the Cricut would cut through the material twice especially when your images are just too close to each other, it can catch up with the material and pull the material. You wouldn't want this to happen so there should be flexible space between images. Especially when you're previewing your mat, this would save the material in the long run and definitely save a lot of stress and headaches.

- You should not be scared of using scissors if there is a knick in the leather.

- Start with all the pieces stretched out. You might decide to fold the longest piece so that there is a converging point at the middle.

- Hold that middle with your E6000 glue and a binding clip.

- You might have made more than one bow what you need right now is to arrange the longer pieces.

- Apply some glue at the back of the middle position and stick your bow to it. Make sure that you secure that position with a binding clip.

- Allow it to dry for some minutes before we take the next step

- Put some of the E6000 on the barrette and place that back piece on it.

- Apply the glue to that small middle piece of yours. Fold it over the bow at that mid-point till it reaches the back of the barrette.

- Hold it down again with the binding clip and allow what you have done to dry for some hours before you stick them into your hair so that there wouldn't be any case of a bow sticking to the hair.

- Simple huh? You can gift this to your child, and you can also make use of it sometimes. But instead of gifting it to her, both of you should work on it together. Wouldn't that be fun?

36 Pop-up Butterfly Card

The next project here is a little different from what we have been doing. I would like to work on regular conventional designs. This project is a Pop-up butterfly card which is good for a Mother's Day celebration, summer birthdays and anyone who loves butterflies.

There are several versions of this card because obviously there are several butterflies. However, for all versions, you will need the following items:

- A 65 Ib. cardstock which should be in the complementary or opposing colors. You should have 1-3 sheets of the wings; a sheet meant for the outside of the card while the other sheet is meant for the inner part.

- Cricut machine for cutting out your butterfly.

- Adhesive spray. The 3M spray mount is preferred here.

Instructions:

The first thing here unlike other projects is that you should cut out your cardstock. And the only way you can do this is to work on it from your design space. Working on a butterfly is not easy. I must confess, but there are over 50,000 patterns, shapes, and objects to guide you into making that perfect shape. The beautiful thing is that you can check online, understand how it is constructed or you download the file online and work on it. Any way you choose, just make sure you have that butterfly ready. Mine was something like this.

After cutting these intricate pieces. They look so much like the picture below:

I know you're probably thinking how would I be able to do this? First, you can start with the simple versions. Just get two halves of the butterfly together then you can wrap that outer card all around them. Make sure you make use of an adhesive spray to stick the rectangle sections from the slotted butterflies to that outer card but be careful as you do because you wouldn't want to get any glue on the wings.

You may be thinking of assembling the fantasy butterfly or something more like a monarch butterfly. The first thing you should consider doing is to set the butterfly aside and spray them very well; then they should be an interval of 30 seconds before you move to the next process.

This process requires you to place the inner rectangle sections on those slotted butterfly wings while watching the way you place them in the middle top-to-bottom so that they don't overlap on the body of the beauty.

Put the wing color pieces on the butterfly wing. You may decide to choose the fantasy rainbow butterfly you would use one full wing piece.

For the monarch butterfly, you would use six butterfly pieces which would all fit in together like that puzzle. Just note the way you place these pieces so that you'll position them well perfectly. Keep covering those areas and do the same for the second wing.

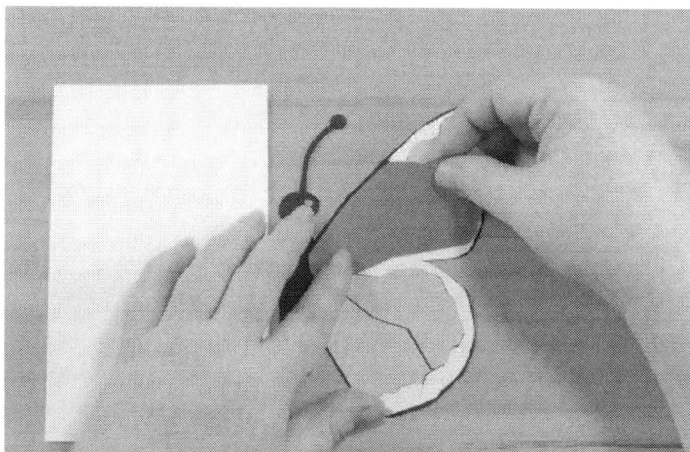

When you have the wing color in place, you should spray the final wing pieces also with the adhesive which you've been using right from time to cover the colored wing. Make sure that you line up the back wing so that it would sync with your pattern.

You'll be required to hold the assembled wings where the body of the butterfly meets the rectangle.

Each part should be slotted together side by side from one side then to the other from top to bottom.

What is followed next? You place that outer card. How can you do this? First, you fold the butterfly and put the small black butterfly cuts you have gotten from the Cricut back into their positions. Doing this would allow you to protect the inner cardstock especially when the next step comes on.

Protect the wings with some of your scrap paper. I made use of blue scrap paper in the picture below. So, you can spray both the front and back of that your folded piece.

The next process if for you to remove the black butterfly inserts that shows some white butterflies also. Then you line up the outside card with those pretty looking butterflies so that all the butterfly's images are all lined up perfectly.

Place the black and orange butterfly into those empty spaces that are present on the front of the card so that it covers the adhesive card beneath it.

Don't forget to be creative by adding extra butterfly inserts inside the card also. The most beautiful thing about this is that you can create that 3 D effect by folding the butterfly up a little bit. The process may seem to be very complex but trusts me; it's worth your time.

37 Snowflakes

Materials:

- The Cricut machine

- Holographic Iron-on vinyl

- Pressing iron

- White glitter iron-on vinyl

- Blue felt

- Twine

- A snowflake SVG file which you upload to the design space

Instructions:

The Ornament

- Edit the design into about 4 inches in diameter; remove all visible lines and layers.

- Arrange the background on which the felt layer will be put.

- Build the upper layer on which the holographic iron vinyl will sit.

- Prepare the green leaf appearance to be placed on the white glitter iron-on vinyl.

- Go with the prompts on the screen in cutting the designed layers.

- Prepare a 12-inch twine and put it on the felt close to the position of the snowflake.

- Press the holographic iron-on vinyl, ensuring that the twine lies perfectly in the middle of the vinyl, and the blue felt as you apply the pressure with the pressing iron.

- Place the white glitter iron-on vinyl on it and iron it.

- Make an elegant little bow with the twine in its position right on the snowflake.

The Card

- Prepare an envelope and card.

- Get a silver glitter vinyl that fits perfectly to the shape of the card.

- Put the cut vinyl on the card.

- Make a hole using a paper punch on the card.

- Get the prepared ornament and fix it onto the front of the card, making use of the twine and secure it firmly into place. You can also make use of an adhesive to hold it.

38 Halloween Spiders

Materials:

- SVG Spider web file

- Cricut machine

- Adhesive

- Black paper

- Pieces of parchment paper

Instructions:

- Place the SVG file into the Design Space and proceed to cut into different web sizes.

- Place the parchment papers on the work area.

- Arrange the spider web just how you want it to look on the worktable.

- After the arrangement of the web, move onto joining the edges of the webs with your adhesive. You have to be careful here to make sure that you get only the edges joined together.

- Wait for a few minutes to get it properly dried.

- Hang it around the house, and you have your perfect Halloween Spider web design!

39 Herringbone Themed Wall Anchors

Materials:

- Cricut machine
- Vinyl
- Pine board (12" width)
- Hooks
- Wax
- Finish paint
- Drill
- Screws
- Foam brushes

Instructions:

- Sand, the pine board, then put on a coat of your favorite stains. Make use of foam then bush with a rag to apply it evenly.

- Go into your design space and get the herringbone design. This pattern is most likely available on your stencil.

- Design the pattern to fit in with the width of your pine board and possibly the length of the board if you want it to cover the entire surface or maybe just halfway or any length you so desire.

- When you are done, tap on the "GO" icon on the user interface from which you will proceed to the preview window.

- Go with the prompts that come up.

- Load up the vinyl and the mat.

- Ensure that the machine is set to vinyl.

- Tap on the GO button.

- After the cutting process is done, remove the cut material from the machine, and then place it on the pine board.

- Coat the cutting on the board with your choice of paint and allow it to dry.

- Remove the vinyl cutting and then sand it a little again.

- Wax the board, allow it to dry, and then use a lint-free cloth to buff it up.

- Get some anchors and place in the predrilled holes on the board before hanging it up on the wall.

40   Customized Letterboard

If you want to step up your game with Cricut, you can try and make a customized letterboard. This project can make a great gift for anyone or can pose as a great addition to your own living and working space. Let's see what you need to make this adorable project.

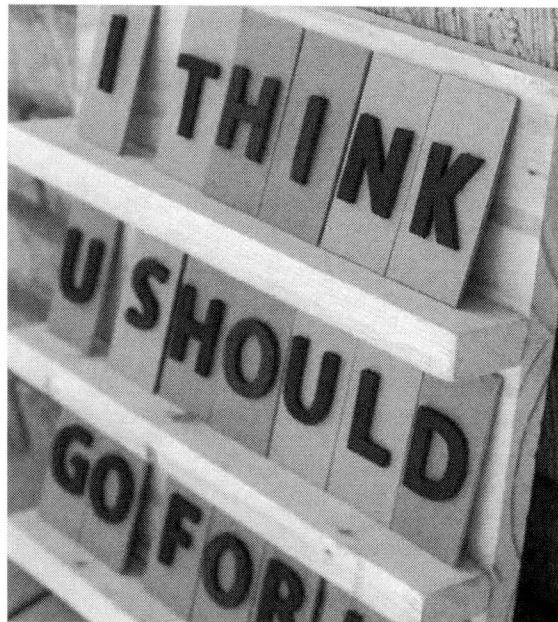

Materials:

- 12x12 Pine board

- 1x2 boards – 12-inch cut

- 12x18 Cricut craft foam

- Cricut chipboard

- Painters tape

- Glue gun

- Cricut machine

Instructions:

First, you will start a new project and upload the SVG pattern for letters or make your own letters for cutting by choosing a font, style and the size of the letters. Each letter shouldn't be larger than a couple of inches. You will also be making little boards for every letter. You can make as many letters as it can fit on a single piece of craft foam. You will be able to change letters and create new statements as you like by changing the letters on the board and storing away the ones you are not using. Make sure to set the line type for the letters for cutting.

Once you have all the letters you need, the font you like and the size you want, you can proceed to cut the first part of the finishing design. Click on "Make it" and specify the material to crafting foam. Make sure to check if all letters are cut through as you might need to give the material a second pass through the blade.

You will get more than a handful of foam letters to work with after you remove the letters from the material by cuts:

Once all letters are cut out and removed from the foam piece, you can start designing supporting boards for letters in the shape of a rectangle. Click on "Shapes" to pick a rectangle. After that, you can select the shape and duplicate it multiple times so that the number of boards matches the number of letters you have. Make sure to make the boards a little wider than the size of the letters. For "M" and "W", you will need bigger boards. Make sure that the size of your letters can fit the size of the letter boards, while the letters should have extra room when attached to the board.

You will be using the Cricut chipboard as your material of choice for the letter boards. Make sure to set the line type for the rectangles to "Cut". Alternatively, instead of using shapes for the board design, you can divide a layer in Canvas sized to fit the size of the chipboard, so that the lines are defining rectangles. The line type should be set to cutting. Proceed to "Make it" and specify material preferences to the Cricut chipboard. You won't be able to use chipboard in case you are using any other model of Cricut aside from Maker.

The letters are ready and so are the supporting boards, which means it is time to get to gluing. Use hot glue or a glue gun to attach the letters to the backing boards made of chipboard. You can then use the letters to assemble statements on your letterboard. There is only one thing left to do before we can say the project is done - creating a board for your letters. You will do this by using a 12x12 inch board as specified in materials and 1x2 strips of wood (12 inch length).

Measure the board so you could "divide" it with three wooden strips – this is where you will be placing your letters to form witty statements. Use glue to attach the strips to the board. Let the glue dry and your board is ready to be used. You can paint the board if you like and pick any color for the materials you are using so that you can give your project a personalized and unique look.

41 Customized Shoes

You can customize shoes and sneakers with Cricut tools and appliances such as Cricut machine and Cricut Easy Press, yes! That means that you can step up your game and start making little fashion wonders out of plain regular shoes. This project will surely give you an insight into how professional Cricut crafting may look like. Selling customized goods? This is where you can start considering crafting as a valid option when it comes to your profession. Let's see what you need to get started with this super interesting project.

Instructions:

- Canvas shoes in any color (we recommend white)

- Cricut Iron-on (colors of your choice)

- Cricut Easy Press (mini version would work the best) – you can also use a regular iron – small iron would be perfect

- Weeding tool

- Cricut machine

Materials:

- First you want to make sure that your patterns for shoes are ready and that you have canvas shoes to work with. You can download free patterns like sprinkles or animal prints that you can use on vinyl to customize the shoes. You can also make your own designs in Design Space. Make sure to arrange the line type to "Cut" when you are done with designing and before you send your design to cut. You can also browse through the Image library and search for suitable patterns there. Use the search bar to narrow down your searches and become more efficient.

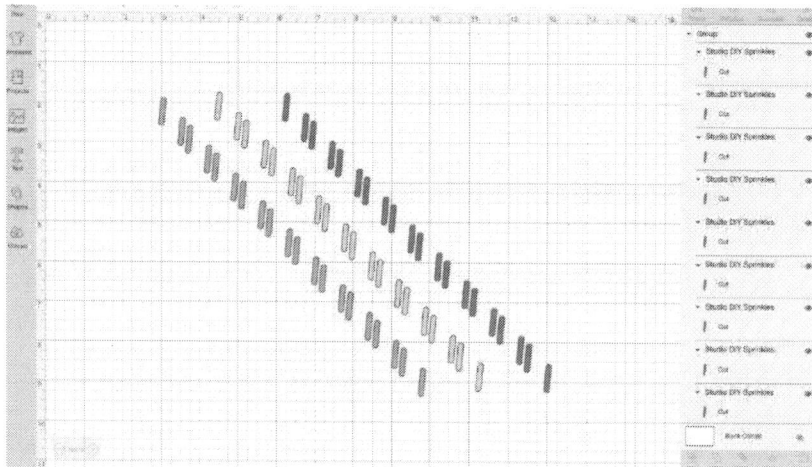

- This is how you can make a pattern for sprinkles for your iron-on. Make sure to size the elements to your preferred proportions and also prepare the design by clicking on "Mirror" – remember to use this command for designs that include iron-on vinyl. Once your design is ready, click on "Make it" and specify the material you are using – iron-on vinyl (Cricut iron-on).

- If you want to make a design for the entire front part of the shoe, you can create your pattern to fit the size of the shoes you are using, instead of applying vinyl in bits:

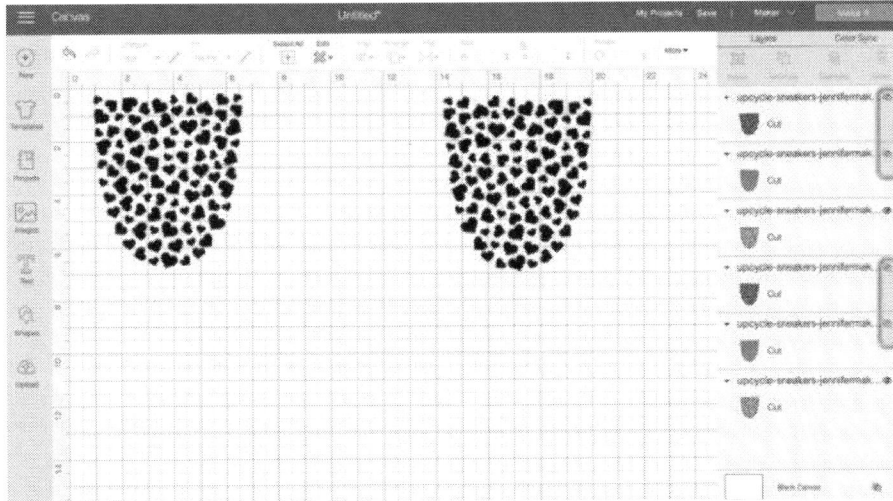

- Load your Cricut machine with vinyl – to fixate the vinyl, you can use tape to attach the edges of vinyl to the cutting mat. Once your design is cut out, use the weeding tool to peel off the excess vinyl and bits of vinyl and so that you bare left with your design. You can use the trick from the first chapter – tip #21 – setting the "Make it" material preferences to "Cardstock" instead of choosing iron-on vinyl or "Everyday Iron-on". That way, you won't need to use the weeding tool to clean the excess vinyl from smaller pieces of the pattern. Now that your design is ready, it is time for the third step.

- It's right about time to give your iron or Easy Press a go. Heat the press and set the temperature to medium. Place a sock inside of the shoe to make a support and protect your fingers – the press and iron can burn your fingers by heating the canvas of the shoe – the sock is both practical and serves the purpose of taking precautions against potential burns. Place the vinyl by bits, one at a time, or as you find suitable based on your design.

- Put the press/iron over the vinyl part and on the canvas while holding the support from inside the shoe. Make sure to avoid other parts of the shoe other than canvas, like the rubber edges for example. Press against the canvas and vinyl for 20 seconds with a press/iron. Do not remove the protective sheet from the vinyl parts until you have pressed and heated the entire design. Once you are done with ironing/pressing, you can remove the sheets. Keeping the sheets on the design while ironing will protect the design from heat and keep it intact. You have your shoes ready to be worn, gifted or for sale.

42 Customized Coffee Cups

- Ever wanted to make your own personalized coffee cups – Starbucks style? If you like your coffee and if you like designing (which you most definitely do), you will love this project. Personalizing coffee cups, although fun, may require some advanced skills and we are sure that you have everything in control there. So, let's see what we need to get started with personalized coffee cups, Starbucks style.

Materials:

- Adhesive vinyl – permanent

- Cups – any type would work; you can buy reusable cups in bulks and get some in the size of Starbucks cups.

- Transfer tape

- Weeding tool

- Cricut machine

Instructions:

- Find and download, then upload SVG files for Starbucks-style cups or make your own to fit the Starbucks aesthetic.

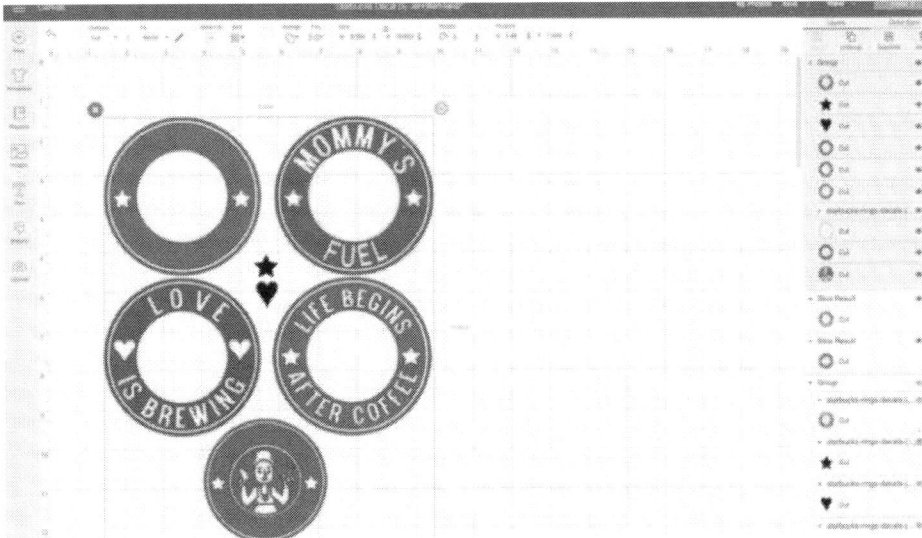

- You can also make your own by using shapes and designing tools in the Design Space. Make sure to measure the cups so that the personalized logo you are making is proportional to the size of the cup you are planning to customize. You can use shapes and letters with editing tools to make your own designs. Letters can be rotated to fit the shape of the circle design and you can use any font you like, write names or funny and witty statements. Make sure to set the line type for designs to "Cut". Once you are ready with editing and/or designing, you can click on "Make it" to proceed to cut. Specify vinyl as your material of choice when adjusting settings for cutting.

- It's time for weeding. Take your weeding tool and remove the parts of vinyl that you don't need in your design. Attach the transfer tape to the vinyl, and size the transfer tape to fit the size of the design you will use on the cup. Apply the vinyl with transfer tape on the cup and smooth the tape out to remove the bubbles. You can use a spatula for that, but your fingers would also do the work. Remove the transfer tape and your customized cup is good to go!

43 Glasswork and Glass Etching

- Customizing glassware with etching? "Do tell more!", right? Imagine all the possibilities you have with etching as a technique and with the Cricut machine as your first and most important helper. You can customize any type of glassware, which includes glass mugs and cups and other glassware such as glass bowls and similar. Here is everything you need from start to finish so you could begin with etching glassware masterpieces.

Materials:

- Vinyl
- Stencil
- Transfer tape
- Glassware of your choice
- Etching cream
- Spatula
- Weeding tool
- Painting brush

Instructions:

- Upload SVG file with shapes and silhouettes you want to use for your glassware or find some designs you like in the library of images you have in the Design Space. You will need to resize or size the pieces to fit the size of your glassware and the part of the glassware you want to apply the vinyl to. Once the shapes are done and sized, you will need to set the line type to cut and choose vinyl as your material of choice after clicking on "Make it". Load the machine and fixate the vinyl piece before cutting.

- Once the design is cut out and ready, you will need to weed excess parts with the weeding tool. Weed out the positive part of your design – the inside of the design, so you are left with a pattern and substantial amount of vinyl around the shape. Next, you will apply the transfer tape on the piece of vinyl with the design pattern. Apply the tape with the vinyl on the glassware and smooth it out across the surface. Remove the transfer tape from the glassware.

-

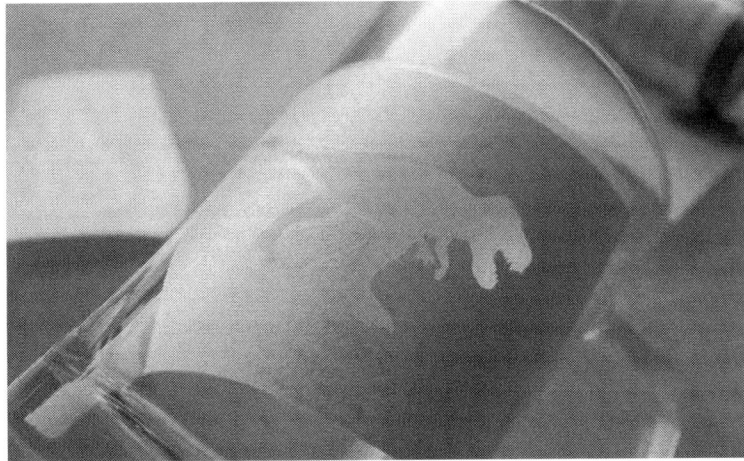

- Use the etching gel by applying it over the cutout part of the design and don't be afraid to use more etching glue as you want it to stick there. You will remove the excess gel later with a spatula. Before removing extra gel, you need to let the etching gel to sit for at least 20 minutes. Once the gel has settled, use the spatula to remove most of the gel.

- You don't need to throw your gel as you can reuse it – return it to the container and it will be good to use on more projects. After removing extra gel, remove the remaining gel by washing it with soap and warm water. Peel off the vinyl then give it another go with soap and warm water. Let the glassware dry and you have a masterpiece ready to be displayed and used.

44 Marbled Journal and Vinyl Art

You might remember how we advised you to plan your projects ahead so you would know what to make and what to use for each project out of tools and materials? Why not make a lovely planner with an interesting marbled cover with vinyl art? It sounds like a challenge you are accepting, so let's see what you need to start making your personalized planner.

Materials:

- Gold foil vinyl

- Marble paint – several colors of your choice

- White paint

- Transfer paint

- Disposable foil pan – to fit the notebook

- Kraft paper notebook

- Weeding tool

- Cricut machine

Instructions:

- For the first step you will leave the Design Space waiting as you are going to prepare the notebook and complete marbling first. Combining multiple crafting techniques is essential to becoming an advanced crafter, which is how you will make great use of this project. In case the cover of the notebook you are going to use for the project has a logo or images on it, use a layer of white paint to cover it up before marbling the cover with paint.

- Let the layer of white paint dry for a while as you are preparing the foil pan and marble paint. Fill up the foil pan with water then add the colors – only a drip or two of each color would be enough. Pour the paint drips in the center of the foil pan filled with water. Prepare the paper towels and sink the cover of the notebook into the foil pain. Hold it for a couple of seconds until the cover gets all the colors on, then place the paper towel between the cover and paper to prevent the water drops from reaching the paper inside the notebook.

119 | P a g .

- Let the marble paint on the cover dry as you are starting the Design Space and preparing vinyl for cutting.

Start a new project in the Design Space and upload the SVG file for letters and patterns you want to use on your notebook cover. You can also create your own design by using shapes, images, and letters available in the Design Space. Change the line type to cut once your design is ready. Set vinyl as your material of choice after you click on "Make it". Send the design to cutting after loading your machine with gold foil vinyl.

Use the weeding tool for removing the negative part of the vinyl design – the background. Peel off the bigger parts of the vinyl and scrape the rest with the help of your weeding tool. Apply the transfer tape on the vinyl design - make sure to size the transfer tape to fit the vinyl design. Apply the transfer tape with vinyl on the cover of the notebook. Smooth out the tape to remove any bubbles then remove the tape. You have just made your personal planner or an amazing gift for someone.

45 Candle Lantern

- Yes, you can make a lantern with your Cricut machine! This is perhaps one of the most exciting projects we have collected for Cricut crafting and it really shows the potential of Cricut and endless possibilities you get with your machine and blades. Check out what you need to get started and try and make this lovely lantern.

Materials:

- Cricut Metallic Poster Board

- Cricut Chipboard

- Hot Glue

- Candle – you can use a small lamp as an alternative

- Cricut machine

Instructions:

- You need to download and upload SVG project file for Cricut Design Space, or make your own latticework in the Canvas (for the latticework) and frames for the lantern that would be made of chipboard. Start a new project and upload your SVG pattern, or start making your own.

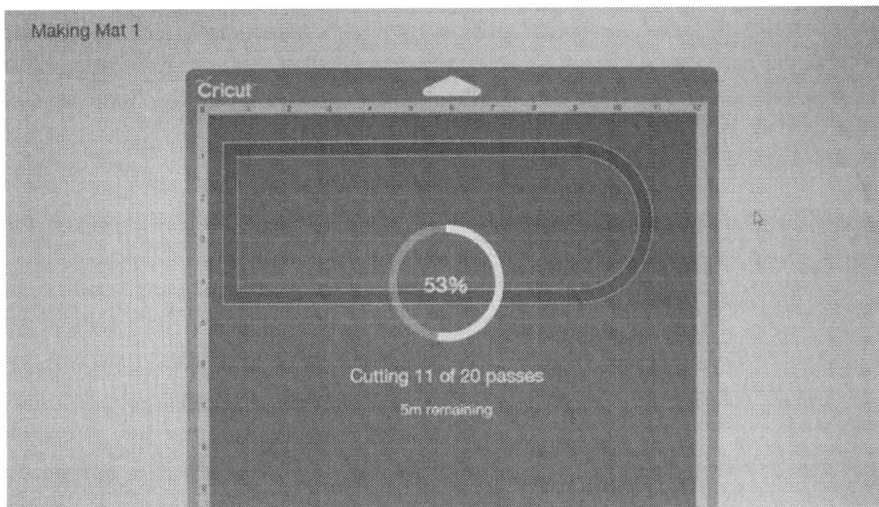

The frames should look like so:

- You only need to make one and cut it 8 times as you will need 8 pieces of the frame cut out of chipboard. The cutting will take some time as you need to make 20 passes for each piece. It may even take an hour until you cut them all out and prepare them for latticework.

- When the frames are all cut out and there are 8 pieces, you will start making patterns for latticework, or find SVG pattern online or in the library of images in the Design Space. Make sure that the width and length of the lattice piece fit the size of frames so that you don't need to manually recut the latticework before attaching lattice to frames. The latticework may look like so:

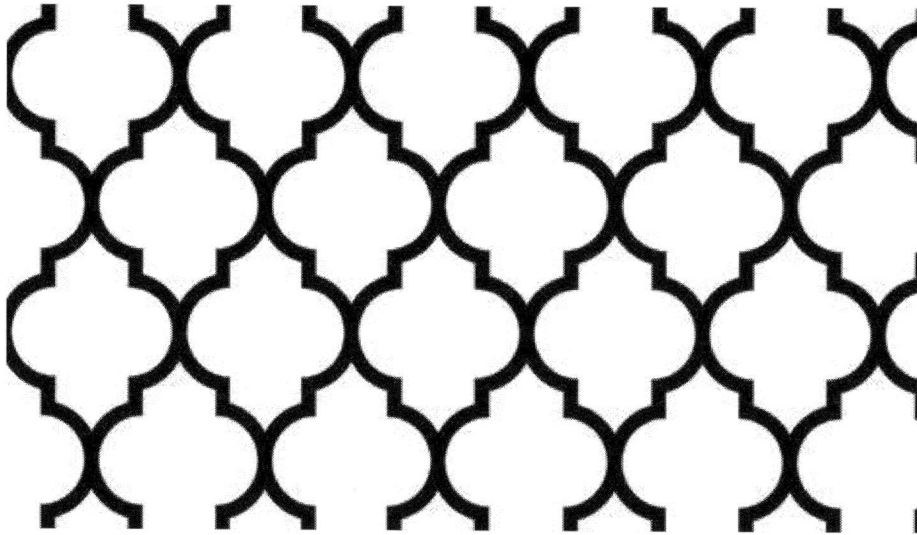

- You can also make the design tighter and play with shapes and lines to create your own patterns. In the image above, you can see a Moroccan quatrefoil, but you can use any pattern for lattice that you like and prefer. Once you are done with the latticework in the Canvas, set up the material preferences to Cricut Metallic Poster Board under "Make it" and load the machine with the specified material.

- The lattice should be cut with Fine Point blade, while Chipboard should be cut with the Knife blade – make sure to always check which blade fits the type of material you are using. Also, make sure to calibrate your blades when using them for the first time.

- It's time to glue and assemble all parts. So, you should have four equal lattice pieces - one lattice piece for two frames. First, add some glue inside the frame and over the edges. Attach the latticework and make sure it fits the frame. Add glue to another frame then assemble the piece with a lattice to the second frame. Repeat that for the remaining three sets of frames and lattice pieces. Glue the four pieces together to form a box and you have a wonderful piece of decorative art for your home or as a gift to someone.

Other Projects Ideas List:

Project 0 — Cricut Face Mask

Project 1 — A Simple Birthday Card

Project 2 — "Welcome to Our Happy Home" Sign

Project 3 — "Queen B" T-shirt

Project 4 — Personalized Paper Bookmark

Project 5 — Fancy Leather Bookmark

Project 6 — Personalized Envelopes

Project 7 — Clear Personalized Labels

Project 8 — Stenciled Welcome Mat

Project 9 — "Momma Bear on Board Keep Your Distance" Car Window Stickers

Project 10 — Car Keys, Wood Keyring

Project 11 — Simple Clothing Labels

Project 12 — Name and Kiss Glitter Tumbler

Project 13 — Sleep Eye Mask with Eyes

Project 14 — Pet Name Collars

Project 15 — Cricut Foil Streamers

Project 16 — Temporary Tattoos

Project 17 — Non-Slip Fun Socks with Heat Transfer Vinyl

Project 18 — Party Plates

Project 19 — Hologram Party Box Tumblers

Project 42 — Recipe Stickers

Project 43 — Wedding Invitations

Project 44 — Custom Notebooks

Project 45 — Paper Flowers

Project 46 — Crepe Paper Bouquet

Project 47 — Leaf Banner

Project 48 — Paper Lollipops

Project 49 — Paper Luminary

Project 50 — Paper Boutonniere

Project 51 — Project Ideas By Craft

Project 52 — Paper Crafts

Project 53 — Adhesive Vinyl Crafts

Project 54 — Iron-On Vinyl Crafts

Project 55 — Wood Crafts

Project 55 — Fabric Crafts

Project 56 — Felt Roses

Project 57 — Custom Coasters

Project 58 — Customized Doormat

Project 59 — T-Shirts (Vinyl, Iron On)

Project 60 — 3d Paper Flowers (Paper)

Project 61 — Luminaries

Project 62 — Earrings

Project 86 — Paper Wall

Project 87 — Piñatas

Project 88 — cardstock

Project 89 — Towel

Project 90 — Christmas bulbs

CHAPTER 6:

Tips and Techniques

Design Canvas Platform

1. Tailor the projects to Hammer, Contour, and Slice. Every file, whether it is from the Design Space Photo Library or one you create yourself, can be modified constantly, edited and customized using the three key editing tools: Weld, Contour, and Slice. Both three of these devices are situated around the right-hand toolbar at the lower end.

   They will only illuminate when the features are required for a particular style. Such devices might not look like they do anything at first sight. They are though extremely effective and are the keys to customizing the projects.

2. Test with Your terms of search. I've learned that the Design Space Image Library search function can be somewhat unique. A fairly standard word which I think does sometimes not produce all kinds of pictures. Yet if I adjust a single phrase or even a single letter, more photos will suddenly appear. As such, I suggest that you play around with lots of web searches to figure exactly what is needed.

3. See the Same Cartridge for details. Using the search feature, you can find a picture you want within an entire host of other photos you don't. What do you do if you want to see more photos that are closely related to the one you desire? The appropriate way to continue is with the cartridge (set) from which it came. To view the cartridge rapidly and conveniently, just click on the tiny details circle (i) in the right-hand bottom corner of each image in the Design Space Photo Library (below left). With a clickable (green) connection, it will open the picture information, which will take you to the complete range of photos (below right).

4. Nonetheless, I understand that most people, particularly newbies, do not want to invest time on their machines just to exercise cutting, certainly not at first. If you're just finding your way around, want to see your computer in motion, and want to reduce your drafting costs as low as possible, make sure to use the Cricut Modeling Room FREE tools. To locate FREE images... use the Filter in the Picture Library of Design Space. Simply pick the "Free" option to view an assortment of photos that you can attach at no expense to your projects!

5. Quickly re-color. The Color update tool is a way to save time on your projects and make certain that you use identical colors across various designs. When putting multiple designs on the Design Canvas, you can end up with different colors of the same hue (e.g., 3 various green-color types, 4 various blue-color types, etc.). Rather than choosing each layer for them to be colored again, move through the right-hand tool panel to the Color Sync feature...

   In this feature, all the various colors you are using when making projects can be seen, dragging, and dropping all layers on your templates to a different color being depicted can be achieved. It is a fast and easy method if you want to allow your colors to be consistent in all of the designs you are making, or you want a specific layer to have a unique color so that your cutting can be more efficient.

6. The Hide Tool. I also take hundreds and loads of pictures to play with while I am carrying out work. Even so, I don't ever have to cut anything on my canvas when it applies to my designs to be carved out. There are even occasions that I only have to cut or try cutting a portion of the template. Instead of erasing photos from my canvas specifically to avoid cutting them, I will "hide" them by tapping the eye icon next to the precise photo on the Layers panel on the right. Any "secret" photo isn't deleted from your board, but it won't be used while you're submitting the idea to be sliced. The "Cover" icon turns on or off, making it so simple to cut what you want or hold your canvas without losing sight of pictures you may still want to play with!

7. Change to Cut, Score, or Draw any line. Once upon a time, whether you chose to draw or rank a line (rather than cut), you 'd have to choose a pattern with certain special characteristics. Nevertheless, a new update to Design Space now makes it easy to adjust every line from cut to score to draw with the basic drop-down Linetype menu at the top toolbar:

8. Tamper with trends. You can now also adjust how the picture is filled in along the top toolbar with the latest Fill tool. You may switch colors or allocate a template to the inside of the photo with an individual section picked.

   A nice way of adding passion to your tasks without focusing on striped scrapbook paper or cardstock is to fill the photos with one of the pre-loaded patterns. You can also control the size and direction of the template by tapping on "Edit Template" in the Design menu (under Fill), in relation to the uncountable options that are available.

   NOTE: You can only use the template choice via the Print-then-Cut technique.

9. Use shortcuts on the keyboard. For almost any order you can imagine about, there are buttons on the Design Space canvas (e.g., Duplicate, Remove, Print, Cut, Paste, etc.) Such buttons appear in the edges of the photos themselves, in the top toolbar, and the right-hand Layers Panel. Remember to use many of the keyboard shortcut keys that function in other computer software to save energy, though. In general, these shortcuts are very useful.

   They can save you loads of effort while working on massive projects: copy (control C) Paste (control V) Erase Undo (control Z).

10. Using "Seed Break." One device that may be absent at Cricut Design Space is a crop machine. Yeah, frankly, I have always longed for a device that would allow me to break projects apart quickly and effectively, or trim off those specifics like you do in many other programs. There's one solution, though! To do what a traditional Crop device can do, you should use the Slice Tool in combination with the free forms (e.g., circle, square). It can be a bit tiresome and not user friendly.

Cut Screen Platform

1. Shift things around on the Mat. Keep in mind that you could push the things on the cut screen itself across the mat. Although the app for Design Space will auto-populate the photos into the mats depending on their color and position, it might not be precisely where you like them.

You can push a cut anywhere around the mat merely by clicking and dragging the photos, and sometimes even flip it using the grips at the top right-hand corner.

Not only does this enable you to wrinkle things narrower than the software originally implies, but it also guarantees that your cut is exactly where you want it to be (like when you're trying to use a slab or strangely shaped piece of material). Only make sure that the grid lines on the panel follow the grid lines on your mat to make sure that the design fits your content wherever you have it.

2. Shift photos from one pad to another. While transferring photos along with a single pad, you can transfer every photo from one pad to another (without needing to go back to the canvas of design and adjust the color). Only press on the 3 dots of every picture on your cut mat in the upper left-hand corner. Then pick "Switch to Another Pad"...

3. Disable the Mats and Save. One of the nicest aspects of how Design Space function is that if you submit the concept to cut, you don't have to devote much effort. As far as you load in your printer the correct color and scale paper exactly like it is seen on the left side of your cut panel, your design will turn out how you planned it! You may find, though, that you want to choose the next mat, re-cut a specific mat or bypass a mat completely. Fortunately, it's extremely fast and doesn't need to cut screen exiting. You will selectively pick which mat to be cut next by randomly choosing or clicking it on the left-hand side before loading the mat into the unit. The computer will automatically spring to whatever mat you pick manually.

4. Link many At One Devices. I understand that most people do not own a multi Cricut machine.

Notwithstanding, if you have this machine, using either Bluetooth or USB to link all devices simultaneously into your Design Space profile (account) is attainable. So, don't stress about having the false machine cut the false design out. Your first and only move on the final cut screen is to choose the computer you want to use via the top dropdown menu, no matter how many machines you have attached. This way, you can always be confident that you are using the computer meant for your task!

5. Edit Some Content Cut Parameters. One thing I keep questioning is that I have a lot of downsides about cutting appropriate materials. Even with the device is a set to Vinyl, for instance, some people have informed me their Cricut won't cut through it completely. Luckily, the parameters for any material (including size, edge, and how many passes the tool can make) can be changed straight from the Materials screen.

Here's how it works:

The 'materials' is an option you should choose, it is visible and can be seen on the 'cut display' (your Explore machine dial should be set to 'custom' if the Maker is not what you are using)

View all products should be selected next (look at the top, you will see some tiny green letters)

Tiny letters that are green in color can be seen down below; it reads as 'material settings'

Any of your choice materials can be selected in this setting; the settings can also be adjusted... this is inclusive of a couple of moves that should be made by the device and how intensive each pass should be.

6. Cut Pressure quickly changes. Although it's great to be able to change some material's parameters, often you only need a little more or a little less friction to make the material sliced through smoothly. To do this, after selecting your material on the final cutting screen, change the force to be either Default, More or Less using the dropdown menu:

It is a perfect way to get the cutting depth correct easily and accurately without needing to run into the design settings!

7. Fill Mat Through Adjusting Copies of Works. I'll admit that one of my favorite parts from the old Cricut machines is no longer available: Autofill. I loved putting a single star on my design canvas, picking my paper size, and then clicking "Autofill." The computer would then load my poster with as many stars as it could fit perfectly. While this specific function is unavailable from Design Space, the workaround is remarkably simple.

There is an alternative at the upper end of the very first cut screen to set your "Project Copies." This feature involves cutting as many durations as you want with whatever is on your design canvas.

8. Set the Cut Screen to Mirror. There will be occasions, particularly when you're planning to work on Iron-On ventures, that you'll need to reverse-cut the design (aka: Mirror). Even though you can switch your design onto the design canvas horizontally, there is currently an option on the cut screen itself to Replicate your designs: This not only helps you to replicate just the mats and photos you need to be rotated over but also helps in creating and modify the un-flipped version on the design screen (which is much pleasant to focus at and personalize).

9. Instructions Fool-proof. One of the favorite features to take the time on the cut screen to pick your personalized material is that Design Space will give you a lot of extremely useful reminders to make sure that your tasks are perfect. For starters, when you choose "Iron-On," Mirror your designs will be reminded, and the glossy side of your vinyl will be put on the mat.

Learning to use the "Cricut" machine definitely involves a steep learning curve. The more complicated aspect of it all is using the "Design Space" software to hone down a variety of features and tools to help you craft your designs and turn your "inspiration into creation". There are multiple shortcuts on the "Design Space" application to make your designing not only easy but more efficient. Let's look at some of the tips and tricks that will make your creative self-stronger and happier!

"Design Space" Application

- The "Weld", "Contour" and "Slice" functionalities to customize your designs. These 3 tools will be activated at the bottom of the screen for designs that allow for these changes.

- The "Weld" tool will allow you to merge two different designs to obtain one composite design, without any leftover seams and cut lines that might be present on the individual designs. This helps you in obtaining single continuous cuts for your design so you do not need to glue and assemble multiple pieces to obtain the final design, for example, creation of cake toppers, gift tags and other decorations.

- The "Contour" tool can be used to activate or deactivate any cut lines in any cut files and thereby allowing you to customize the image in various ways. So imagine you have an image of a flower and you want to remove the details of the design and obtain more of an outline of the flower, you can do so by clicking on the "Contour" button at the bottom of the screen and selecting the different elements of the image that you want to turn on or off from the contour pop-up window.

- The "Slice" tool can be used to slice a design from an image by cutting out or removing elements of the image, as shown in the picture below.

- Use your search keywords wisely. The search functionality within the "Design Space" is not very dynamic so your choice of keywords will make a big difference on the designs and projects that will be displayed to you. For example, if you search for images containing dotted designs and search with keyword "Dots", you would be given around 120 images but if you search with the term "Dot" you would see almost twice as many images. You should also search with synonyms and closely related terms of your target project idea. For instance, if you wanted to create a Halloween project, you can search with terms like pumpkin, costumes and trick or treat among others. This will ensure you are viewing all images pertaining to your project.

- The "Cartridge" image sets. It is likely that during your search, you like a design more than any other made available to you but it is not exactly how you want it to be. Well, simply click on the small information circle at the bottom of the image and you will be able to view the entire image set or "cartridge" of images similar to your selected image within the "Design Space Image Library".

- A treasure trove of free fonts and images. As a beginner you would want to make use of the large number of free fonts and images to get hands-on experience with your "Cricut" device. This is a great way to spend less money and still be able to create stunning craft projects. Within the "Design Space" application, you can click on the "Filter" icon next to the search bar (available within the images, fonts and projects tabs) and select "Free" to only view free resources within each category.

- Use synchronized colors to save time and money. This is a great tool when you have designs that are either a composite of multiple images or inherently contains different hues of the same color. Instead of using 5 different shades of the same color, you can synchronize the colors, so you need to use only one colored sheet. To do this, simply click on the "Color Sync" tab on the "Layers Panel" on the top right corner of the screen. Then drag and drop desired layer(s) of the design to your target color layer and the moved layer will immediately be modified to have the same color as the target color.

- Use the "Hide" tool to cut images from the Canvas selectively. When you are looking to turn your imagination into a work of art, you may want to view and take inspirations from multiple images while you work on your design. But once you obtain your desired design you would not want to cut every other image on your canvas. This is where the "Hide" tool comes in handy, so you do not need to delete the images on the Canvas to avoid cutting them along with your project design. To hide the image, you just need to click on the "eye" symbol next to those specific image layers on the "Layers Panel". The hidden images will not be deleted from the Canvas but would not appear on the cutting mat when you click the "Make It" button to cut your project.

- Ability to change the design lines to be cut, scored or drawn. With the latest version of the "Design Space" application, you have the ability to simply change the "Linetype" of a design from its predefined type to your desired action, instead of looking for designs that have predefined line type meeting your project need. For example, if your selected design is set at "Linetype" Cut but you want the design to be "Linetype" Score, you can easily change the "Linetype" by clicking on the "Linetype" drop-down and making your selection.

- The power of the "Pattern" tool. As you have learnt from the last project of this book, "Personalized Fridge Magnets", you can use your own uploaded images to be used as pattern fill for your designs. Moreover, you will also be able to edit the image pattern and the patterns that already exist within the "Design Space" application to create your own unique and customized patterns. The "Edit Pattern" window allows you to adjust the resolution and positioning of the pattern on your design and much more. (Remember, to use the "Pattern" feature you must use the "Print then cut" approach for your project, with access to a printer).

- Utilize the standard "keyboard shortcuts". The "Design Space" application does have all the required tools and buttons to allow you to edit the images and fonts but if you prefer to use your keyboard shortcuts to edit the image quickly, the "Design Space" application will support that. Some of the keyboard shortcuts you can use include: "Copy (Control + C)"; "Paste (Control + V)"; "Delete (Delete key)"; "Copy (Control + Z)".

- You can utilize the "Slice" tool to crop the image. The "Design Space" application still lacks the "Crop" functionality, so if you need to crop an image, you will need to get creative. A good tip is to use the "Slice" tool along with the "Shapes" to get your desired image.

- Change the position of the design on the cutting Mat. When you are ready to cut your design and click on the "Make It" button, you will notice that your design will be aligned on the top left corner of the mat. Now, if you are using material that was previously cut at its top left corner, you can simply drag and move the image on the "Design Space" mat to meet the positioning of your cutting material. You will be able to cut the image anywhere on the mat by moving the design on that specific position on the mat.

- Moving design from one mat to the other? Yes! You can not only move the design over the mat itself, you can also move the design from one mat to another by simply clicking on the three dots (...) on top of the mat and select "Move to another mat". You will then view a pop-up window where you can select from the existing mats for your project to be used as the new mat for your selected design.

- Save cut materials as Favorites for quick access. Instead of spending time filtering and searching for your cut material on the "Design Space" application over and over, just save your frequently used material by clicking on the star next to the "Cricut" logo on the "Design Space" application to save them under the "Favorites" tab next to the default "All Materials" tab. When you are getting ready to cut your project, under the "Set Material" tab, your "Favorites" material will be displayed on the screen, as shown in the picture below.

- You can store the most frequently used cut materials on the "Cricut Maker". Unlike the "Cricut Explore" series which has dial settings for a variety of commonly used cut materials, the "Cricut Maker" requires you to use a "Custom

Materials" menu within the "Design Space" application that can be accessed using the button on the machine bearing "Cricut" logo, since there is no dial to choose the material you want to cut.

- Choose to repeat the cut of the same mat or skip a mat from being cut altogether. By following the instructions on the "Design Space" and feeding the right color and size of the material to the machine, you will be able to get your design perfectly cut. You can change the order in which the mats are cut, repeat the cut of your desired mat and even skip cutting a mat, if needed. You can do this easily by simply clicking on and selecting the mat you would like to cut.

How to Use Cricut Iron-On

Christmas theme tea towels make a great gift and super fun to make. Here's how you can make one with quick and easy steps by using Cricut Explore Air.

Here's what you will need: Cricut Explore Air, Cricut Design Space, heat transfer vinyl sheet, Cricut Weeder Tool, tea towels, iron

1. Open Cricut Design Space begin a new project, and then use Cricut Design Space Image Library to select any image you want to work with. For this project, use something that relates to Christmas like "Merry Christmas," and then Cricut Design software will insert the image into a new project.

2. Set the Cricut machine for the "Iron on" setting. You can do this by setting the dial to the "Iron on" position. That's it and leave the rest of the work to the machine.

3. Place a sheet of heat transfer vinyl onto the cutting mat, then load it into the Cricut machine and press the cut button. Make sure the image is in a mirror format as the project deals with heat transfer vinyl.

4. When done, remove the excess vinyl piece from the design by using a Cricut Weeder Tool.

5. Then take a tea towel, fold it neatly, then place vinyl on it, cover with another tea towel and iron it until the vinyl has adhered to the fabric of tea towel.

6. Remove the top tea towel, peel away the plastic backing, discard it, and add more embellishment to the towel, such as adding polka dots by using metallic fabric paint in silver and gold color. Before doing this, place a paper beneath the towel as it will serve as a protective layer until paint gets dry.

Conclusion

Congratulations! You made it here! You've just become a professional Cricut user! However, if you find something along the way that needs a review, don't worry, this book will guide you.

This was written to help you realize the built-in capability of the Cricut machine in producing amazing projects. The easy to follow instructions will surely inspire and ignite the innate creativity and the artistic skills within each of us, which are better than the ones being given here.

Using a Cricut machine should not be a new experience for you by now. However, it would be best if you kept an open mind to new updates. Cricut always give their users a lot of options to choose from, so, try as much as possible to carry out extensive research about their products, materials, and subscriptions.

At this stage, we can both agree that Cricut offers a whole lot more than it requires. Do not give up trying to learn how to cut on Cricut machines. Although it might be a little frustrating getting design right sometimes, keep striving to attain perfection. You'll become professional in no time and probably start teaching other people how to use it.

Cricut machines are getting more popular every day. A lot of people prefer Cricut machines for many reasons. Some of the reasons are User-Friendliness: This is one of the major reasons that people choose Cricut machines to do their cutting job. It's easy to use and easy to learn if you have the right resources. Almost anyone can set up a Cricut machine because it is not too complicated. All that a new user needs to do is to follow the straightforward instructions that come with the box.

A lot of individuals like having their gadgets come in cool designs and structures. Cricut machines check this box emphatically, coming with beautiful designs and appearance.

Cricut machines are designed to handle multipurpose tasks. A lot of work can be done on it without stress. You can write, score, and cut with the machine. A lot of Cricut users are yet to reach the maximum level usage. With Cricut, people rarely over-utilize; most people only underutilize.

Never stop doing research. Never stop trying new things. Never, ever stop being creative. The Cricut does not make you any less creative; it just makes the process easier so that you can focus your valuable time and efforts on more important things or personalizing the projects after making the cuts. It takes the tedious work out of your hands and makes everything fun, easy, and fast.

Now that I have given you several ideas of projects that can be completed with the use of a Cricut, you should have more ideas on how to use your new Cricut machine. Each Cricut can do some super impressive creative projects.

The great thing about the Cricut is that you can use it with so many different materials that you will never run out of ideas for crafting and creating beautiful gifts. Perhaps website composition isn't for you; however, this is only one model. You can likewise make your craftsmanship accessible in prints, shirts, scratchpad... and so on. You can go to the visual communication course and produce work of art for gatherings or organizations.

Enjoy your new knowledge of your fantastic machine and give a new project a try. If you are about to start your first project, consider trying one of the beginner projects outlined. For those that have a few cuts under their belt, give one of the alternative projects a try! Have fun, and do not limit yourself. The beauty of the Cricut is the versatility of functions and user-friendly format. Use this to make your life and home and those of your friends and family more exciting and designed!

Everything necessary is a couple of provisions and some simple guidelines, and you can influence everything without exception you too can envision. You don't need to be a specialist, and you don't need to be great at makes. Give the Cricut a chance to do the diligent work for you and love the outcomes!

All the best!

Printed in Great Britain
by Amazon